D1245402

# INNOCENT

## AN OBSCENE MISCARRIAGE OF JUSTICE

## JOHN N. HUFFINGTON

THE OMNIBUS PUBLISHING
BALTIMORE, MD

The Omnibus Publishing, 5422 Ebenezer Rd., POB 152, White Marsh, MD 21226

www.theomnibuspublishing.com

Author Note: I have tried to recreate events, locales and conversations from my memories of them. In order to maintain their anonymity in some instances I have changed the names of individuals and places, I may have changed some identifying characteristics and details such as physical properties, occupations and places of residence.

Publisher Note: Although the author and publisher have made every effort to ensure that the information in this book was correct at press time, the author and publisher do not assume and hereby disclaim any liability to any party for any loss, damage, or disruption caused by errors or omissions, whether such errors or omissions result from negligence, accident, or any other cause.

Book Layout ©2022 BookDesignTemplates.com - Cover Image Photo by Deepak Digwal via https://www.pexels.com/photo/grayscale-photography-of-person-standing-on-big-microscope-3395507/

Bio Image ©Karen Elliot Greisdorf

Ordering Information: email info@omnibuspub.com for special discounts on bulk quantity purchases by corporations, associations, book clubs, schools, and others.

Innocent. An Obscene Miscarriage of Justice / John N. Huffington. -- 1st ed.

ISBN 979-8-9854108-2-2

Library of Congress LCCN - 2022942088

## Dedication

Dedicated to my mother, Clara McNeill Arther Huffington, who always believed and had to go up and represent me in heaven for the truth to finally be exposed.

I have been blessed with an incredible wealth of friends and supporters who have assisted, encouraged, and made my journey possible. I am grateful for each and every single one of you!

Special thanks to my muse, Ann Spangler Clark, for encouraging me with several swift kicks to write this book and for always being there.

To my scribe and encourager, Melissa Payne Metzger, You Rock!

To all of the attorneys, paralegals, support staff and "plus ones" at Ropes & Gray - without whom I wouldn't be here to tell the story - Thank you just isn't enough.

To my editor, publisher, and friend, Wendy Dean - Thank you for believing in me and making this possible.

"You will be demoralized and exhilarated by this book. Wrongful convictions caused by corrupt prosecutors are a sad fact of life and John Huffington brilliantly depicts its devastating human impact. Huffington guides you through the worlds of drug dealing, the legal system, decades in prison, and finally freedom with clear, passionate prose. You will never forget this story." -- **Tom Jackman, Pulitzer Prize winning writer and staff writer for the *Washington Post***

"The incredible story of John Huffington reads like a novel but it's all too true. Egregiously framed and sentenced to death multiple times, this remarkable man survived 32 years in some of the toughest prisons in the world and lived to tell the tale. Through it all, he maintained good sanity, preserved his kind spirit, and emerged as beacon of light and hope. The only thing more remarkable than this book is the man himself! " -- **Jason Flom, American music industry executive, podcaster, philanthropist, founding Board Member of the Innocence Project , and author of *Lulu is a Rhinoceros***

"*Innocent: An Obscene Miscarriage of Justice*, is a gripping, harrowing, and amazing journey of a man, who if not for the pursuit of the truth, and some luck, would be dead today. Instead, John Huffington is alive to tell his story that everyone should read. To ignore what happened to John would be a travesty – something we can never allow to happen again." -- **Martin H. Tankleff, Peter P. Mullen Distinguished Visiting Professor, Georgetown University; Special Counsel to Barket, Epstein, Kearon, Aldea, & LoTurco, LLP and New York State Exoneree**

"John Huffington has a story and his book is an indictment on the legal system that almost killed him. Read this and be changed forever. I know because he slept right next door in a death row cell beside mine. -- **Kirk Bloodsworth is a former Maryland waterman and the** first American on death row exonerated post-conviction by DNA, *Bloodsworth: The True Story of the First Death Row Inmate Exonerated by DNA (2005)* by Tim Junkin

"John Huffington is a gracious, generous man despite every reason not to be. I am so grateful he is sharing his story with us - it is both difficult to hear and essential to listen to."- **Rev. Nadia Bolz-Weber,** *New York Times* **bestselling author**

"Heart-wrenching, infuriating, and one of the most inspiring stories I have ever read. John's raw vulnerability, character, and overall perspective can and will benefit the world at large. I can't imagine one day of John's story...and yet, feel the urge to want to fight for the truth regardless of the circumstances. John's story is a true embodiment of the human spirit to fight for what is right, no matter the adversity." -- **Joe Mechlinski,** *New York Times* **bestselling author of** *Shift the Work*, **speaker, and social entrepreneur**

"John Huffington shares his powerful and compelling life story of an innocent man in prison who undergoes extreme trauma because of a broken justice system. Huffington gives highly visual descriptions that will shake you to your core. Sounds, scents, and sensations become palpable. A gripping story that is a triumphant testament to the human spirit." -- **Wendy Starland, an Artist honored by the Songwriter's Hall Of Fame, Discovered & Developed Lady Gaga**

"*INNOCENCE* is a must-read for anyone interested in what wrongful conviction looks like first-hand. Huffington's searing story of injustice, perseverance, and hope should not be missed." -- **M. Chris Fabricant Director of Strategic Litigation at the Innocence Project, and Author of** *Junk Science and the American Criminal Justice System*

"John Huffington's story is one of extraordinary resilience and can inspire us all to find purpose in the toughest of circumstances. It is an important story for every citizen to read and understand because there are serious flaws in our justice system that affect us all, and there are things we each can do to make things better. In these pages, you will learn from and be inspired by John, through the vulnerable and brave outpouring of his lifetime of fighting for justice." -- **Nancie McDonnell Ruder, CEO of Noetic Consulting, Author of** *Jack and Jill Went Up the Hill: How Senior Marketers Scale the Heights Through Art and Science (2019)*

"Disbelief, fury, grief, and awe are just a few of the emotions that came rushing through while reading John's raw and heart-wrenching story. The amount of courage and resilience that John embodies to sustain his 32-year battle to defend his innocence is not only inspirational, but proves the incredible capacity of the human body, mind, and spirit when pushed to its furthest limits. Every citizen should read *INNOCENT* – a true story of bravery, determination, and honor." -- **Jackie Insinger, Bestselling author of** *Spark Brilliance***, Speaker, and Leadership and Team Dynamics Consultant**

"John Huffington has lived the nightmare -- first sentenced to death, then imprisoned for three decades for two murders in rural Maryland that he always denied committing. His harrowing story, as told in *Innocent: An Obscene Miscarriage of Justice*, reveals how a prosecutor willing to lie and cheat and an incompetent defense lawyer kept him behind bars for decades. Read it and weep." -- **David O. Stewart, author of** *George Washington: The Political Rise of America's Founding Father*

"John's book is a gut-wrenching account of how utterly the criminal justice system can fail, and how excruciatingly difficult it is to overturn a wrongful conviction. But it is also a story of hope and resilience, this incredible man's three-decade-long search for freedom, and his continued search for justice to clear his name. It is a must-read for citizens interested in criminal justice, law students, and, yes, even lawyers to understand what defendants are up against and what this nation does to those we incarcerate and forget." -- **Rabia Chaudry, Pakistani-American attorney and podcast host.** *New York Times* **best-selling author of** *Adnan's Story: The Search for Truth and Justice After Serial*

"John Huffington's story broke my heart – then it made me believe. We all know our criminal justice system is broken, but what does that look like from the inside? John shows us what the system does to a teenager, to a family, to a city. And then he shows us what it takes to overcome. Unforgettable. -- **Chris Wilson, Serial Social Entrepreneur, Storyteller, Artist, Social Justice Advocate, and author of** *The Master Plan*

# Note from the Editor

In May 1981, I was an eight-year-old elementary school student in Virginia. It would be near the end of my 4th-grade year and my biggest memory is the birth of my cousin, April. I was as close to her as my own sister and she would become my youngest child's Godmother. I remember softball season and a trip to the Outer Banks that summer. It was a carefree time. I didn't watch the news or read the paper. Yet a short drive up I-95, a drug-related double homicide took place that made national news.

I never heard of Diane Becker or Joseph "Joe" Hudson. Their shocking deaths were labeled in the Baltimore press as the Memorial Day Murders. During the attack, Diane took several blows to the back of her head that fractured her skull multiple times. Starting behind her ear, the fractures expanded into the base of the skull. She suffered over thirty stab wounds to her back, chest, and neck. The stabbing was brutal enough to leave knife marks on her spine. Joe lay shot five times, on a dirt road miles away. Twice from behind, three from the front, with all but one shot classified as a lethal injury.

I never heard of John Huffington or Deno Kanaras, the co-defendants in the case. Nor did I know of Joseph Cassilly, the prosecutor who put both men away for those murders. May

1981 moved into June and life went on for me. It was normal. I finished high school, went to college, and then on to grad school. I got a job, got married, and had kids. It would be almost forty years later before I first learned about this case and the people involved.

I moved to Maryland in 2001, less than a month before 9/11. Early on I learned that in Baltimore and the metro area, locals used a play-on-words for the phrase "What a small world." A more concise community description is, "Smalltimore." This is how I met John Huffington. One degree of separation, through a mutual friend. This friend and I met for coffee to catch up on life, leaving with intentions to keep in touch. Not a week later she reached out and asked if I published non-fiction, which of course, I do. She asked if she could give my contact information to a man she knew looking for a publisher and I said yes. Little did I know the scope and breadth of the story that would unfold before me.

My first call from John came on or about May 12, 2021. As his story unfolded over the phone, I stopped him and said, "I have to meet you." I asked if he was free the next day. He said, "Well, I'm free now," and out the door, I went. We met at the Inner Harbor and ate lunch outside on a perfect spring day. The more I heard about his story, the more I became convinced he needed to tell it. I felt in awe of the peace he projected compared to me, sitting across from him, listening for the first time. I felt my left eyebrow raise a little more with each new detail he shared, followed by many a "Are you kidding me?!" My brain scrambled to understand. How did our justice system fail this man time after time, and in ways that seemed implausible? I sat dumbfounded at John's lack of anger. I speculated that he must have his days. But his retelling was calm. Not a sliver of the emotion coursing through me was present in his voice, on his face, or in his body language. How could anyone put through such an obscene miscarriage of justice not feel anger?

Instead, John focuses on what he can control. He is currently the Corporate Social Responsibility Director for Holdings Management Company. He serves as the Vice President & COO of the Kinetic Capital Community Foundation, a charitable organization headquartered in Maryland. Additionally, he supports and works in several charitable organizations throughout the state. In particular, John's work helps get food donations and school supplies. He mentors children and leads community clean-ups. In "Smaltimore," if you have a need, ask John. He is an incredible networker and can introduce you to someone in your community who can help. On the off chance he can't direct you right away, he is the friend or coworker of someone who can. John is well-liked and the support in the fight to clear his name is tremendous. You'll find it in over twenty-four letters of recommendation attached to his petition for a Gubernatorial pardon. It includes letters from government officials, coworkers, and a local television reporter. Add to that his lawyers and close personal friends. John is also backed by the Innocence Project. Top it off with a slew of friends, family, and social media personalities. A local musician even wrote a song about John.

In the months following that first call I recorded hours of personal interviews and gained access to 40 years of court records and case files. As you read his story, in his own words, the trial transcripts and court documents support the facts. There is no "he said, she said." Every bit is in black and white and on the record. Also, keep in mind that over 3,000 names appear on the National Registry of Exonerations. Yet, John's name is not among them. He still fights for exoneration and the ability to take back the name stripped from him all those years ago.

# INTRODUCTION

D

o misery and suffering have a smell and taste? My senses were being assailed and it was like nothing I've ever encountered. I'm struggling to make sense of it all. It was a wintry cold, dreary December morning. Handcuffed and shackled, two large correctional officers shuffled me into the bleak and foreboding bowels of the Maryland State Penitentiary. There was a constant sound. An endless din with unidentified smells permeated the senses. There existed a sense of despair and hopelessness. It was palpable and seemed to sweat from the blocks of granite that made up the walls. Walls that saw an excessive amount of violence and depravity, and absorbed hundreds of years of human suffering and misery.

The Maryland Penitentiary (the Pen) opened in 1811. It was a maximum-security prison located on the edge of downtown, Baltimore, Maryland. An iconic landmark whose turrets stood out in the Baltimore skyline. It had an infamous reputation for the cruelty of the guards and the systemic corruption that marred the prison. Numerous incidents of prison unrest, rioting, violence, and murders over the decades solidified its notoriety. It also housed the state's death row and gas chamber.

That's why I was there. In May 1981, I was eighteen years old and arrested and charged with a drug-related, double homicide. A crime I did not commit but a jury still found me guilty of. Seven months later, a judge sentenced me to two death penalties plus twenty-one years. The system wasted no time and transferred me to the diagnostic center of the prison system. This was the entry point to the Maryland prison system located in Baltimore City, across the street from the Pen. The diagnostic center held new inmates to the prison system here for anywhere from six months to a year. This allowed caseworkers time to determine an inmate's security level and what prison they will enter. The diagnostic center was a new building. It was clean, with large cells and huge windows overlooking the city of Baltimore, almost like a hotel. Because of my two death sentences, the caseworkers didn't have much to review. There was no question about where I would go. The next morning officers came to my cell, woke me up, and ordered me to grab my personal property. It wasn't much more than some legal paperwork and toiletry items. They put me into a three-piece which consisted of handcuffs, wrists secured in the "Black Box" to a belly chain, and leg irons. Then they escorted me to the Penitentiary, a complete contrast to my former lodging. It was like stepping back into another era, to a time of castles and dungeons. I went from the suite life to skid row in a matter of minutes.

The whirlwind of events and jail transfers between my arrest and sentencing hadn't allowed me to process my death sentence. There was no one to talk to, no chance to catch my breath. I entered a system that did not care or want to care. I ceased being human. I was no longer John Huffington. I was Inmate #160354, a condemned prisoner on death row.

My guards escorted me to the Administrative Segregation Tier. This was a lockdown tier where confinement to a cell lasted twenty-three and a half hours per day. A cell door opened, my cuffs and leg irons removed, and then the cell door slammed behind me. Not a word passed between me and my escorts. They provided no orientation, no advice, and no instructions. They deposited me in a six-by-nine-foot cell that consisted of a metal bunk and ceramic toilet and sink. There were no fans or air conditioning. These cells would get so hot that inmates would have to sleep on the floor, pressed up against the cell door to get airflow. Meanwhile, the roaches and mice ran over the top of our bodies. As the guards left me there, I felt my thoughts, fears, and confusion overwhelm me. The constant welter of discordant sounds made up of voices, clanging doors, and rattling keys was something I never adjusted to. It became the soundtrack of my life for the next thirty-two years.

In the beginning, I learned a few things. I learned from inmates that worked on the tiers that I would stay in administrative segregation for the next thirty days. During this time the administration evaluated my mental status before placing me in the general population. I learned that I needed to put a plastic water bucket by my cell door every morning and every night if I wanted hot water. Only cold water ran from our sinks. I learned the routine of "feed-up" as the schedule of meals delivered through the slot in our door. I also learned not to talk and not to trust. As the days, months, and years went by, I felt as though I fell through a hole in the ice without a way to reach back up to the world above. I was not seen or heard. Air bubbles escaped, but they were invisible and silent. No one wanted to hear I wasn't supposed to be there, that I was innocent. I was in the Pen, consumed by my own thoughts and trapped in my own head. And no one cared.

Memorial Day weekend, 1981, I was eighteen years old. I looked forward to the start of summer, hanging with friends, and spending a lot of time at my favorite place, the beach. Little did I know it would be a long and grueling thirty-two years, two months, and twenty-eight days before I would ever get the chance to jump into the ocean again.

So many hamster wheels churning in my head. How did this happen?

# CHAPTER 1

I grew up in Churchville, Maryland. It was a small country town. A person could miss it by blinking as they drove through it. We lived in a middle-class neighborhood that centered around a man-made lake. Churchville was a peaceful, idyllic slice of the country with a touch of suburbia. It was the perfect place to raise a family, where my parents built a house and created a home when I was six years old.

I am one of four children, the second oldest. My sister Pam is about two years older than me. My brother Bill is almost two years younger and my sister, Laura, is three years younger. Pam was the straight-A student and the mini-Mom to us all. Bill was multi-talented in building, constructing, and doing anything with his hands. We doted on our baby sister, Laura. She was cute, outgoing, and had a lot of friends. When we were young, we squabbled our share, but for the most part, got along. In my teen years, I rebelled against my parents' rules and curfews. My disorderly conduct upset the household. Both of my sisters maintained good relationships with me but didn't approve of my actions. Pam was my mentor and the one I turned to for advice while Laura was more like me and the one I would hang out and party with. It was more difficult for my brother. I was a bully toward him and didn't treat him well. We would often quarrel and more often than not, I was the cause of it. Our relationship remained troubled and did not improve until the day of my father's funeral almost forty years later.

My father was a mechanical engineer for the government. He worked at Aberdeen Proving Ground while my mother was a stay-at-home mom. They were both scholars. Dad earned a Ph.D., Mom, a master's degree and both were teachers at various points in their life. For my parents, education was of great importance in our house as was being socially conscious. My mother made sure her children remained active in community organizations such as 4-H, where I volunteered as a camp counselor. I also volunteered with her at Meals on Wheels and stayed active in my church's youth group.

I was a skinny, nerdy kid but in my head and heart, I was so much more. Back in fourth grade, an older sixth-grader kept picking on me at the bus stop. There was a large open lot behind our house where most after-school activities happened. The neighborhood kids played sports there. We were the first family in the neighborhood to have an aluminum baseball bat. My mother purchased it for me and my brother. The bus stop was one street over.

After a week or so of enduring this bullying, I went to the bus stop one morning dragging my new bat. The kid saw me coming and thought it was hilarious. I wasn't much bigger than that bat, but I managed to chase him around the bus stop. He stayed out of reach, laughing at me the whole time. He commented, "This kid's got spunk," and that's how I earned my neighborhood nickname, Spunky. At that moment I established my moxie and stood up for myself. The truth was, I wouldn't have hit him or anyone else that day or ever. Yet this type of "spunk" is the essence of who I am. I will stand up for myself and what is right. I will uphold my character if ever called into question.

My taste for entrepreneurship started early in my life. I found out the lady across the street paid more than my mother for chores. I cut her grass and weeded her garden, as it was the more profitable choice. In grade school, I started a candy business. I figured out I could buy bulk candy from stores and resell individual candy to the kids at school for a profit. I earned extra pocket change, and it set the stage for what was to come; bigger ticket items, higher profits, and a bigger business model.

I did well academically and considered myself a bit of a bookworm. I'm a natural speed reader. I visited the local library every week and checked out a maximum of six books. Then I used my siblings' cards to add a few extra books because ten or twelve wouldn't last me the week.

Like most kids, I encountered the drug world in high school. I started out my high school tenure by hanging out with the jocks and connecting with sports. I grew up playing little league baseball and basketball in the recreation leagues. Being of average athletic talent, I wasn't good enough to try out for teams at the high school level. I ran track my first year but settled into becoming a manager for both the JV and the varsity football teams. A glorified water boy, but I enjoyed it. My best friend, Brian Santiago, played on the junior varsity team and we were inseparable since fourth grade. Brian loves to tell the story of my wrong-team water boy incident. There was a Friday night varsity home game where my team wore dark jerseys. After the game, I stayed out late drinking and partying. I wasn't in the best shape the following Saturday morning for the JV game. During a timeout, I ran out on the field with the water bottles. By mistake, I ran to the team wearing dark jerseys, which ended up being the opposing team. With glee, they accepted my offer of Gatorade while my team laughed at me. It took a while for Spunky to live that one down and still, to this day, Brian loves to tell that story.

In tenth grade, I shifted my friend set to the "heads," kids that were into getting high and partying. For me, I started out experimenting. I was kind of a geek, didn't have a steady girlfriend, and wasn't confident in myself. Most of the time I ended up as the third wheel with my friends when we went out. Trying to find my purpose I leaned into my entrepreneurial instincts. I recognized the advantages of buying small quantities of marijuana and hash, then reselling them to make a profit.

At school, I did well up until my junior year of high school. I even took two years of Latin. Back then, accelerated programs didn't exist, so I wasn't challenged or mentored. I grew bored and, as a consequence, dropped out of high school in my junior year, 1978. I waited the requisite three months, then tested for and received my GED. Because my friends were a year older, I went to Ocean City with them for Senior Week in 1979. Afterward, I enrolled in Harford Community College and registered for restaurant and personnel management courses. At home, my focus turned to the party scene. I gained confidence and more acceptance among my peers because I was dealing drugs. None of this went over well with my parents, especially my father.

The strain on the homefront expanded. My parents grew uneasy about the bad influence I was having on my younger brother and sister. I loved my parents but I thought there was a mutual feeling that it would be better if I wasn't around. I became an emancipated adult at seventeen. Then, despite not being old enough, I signed a lease for an apartment in Abingdon, near Bel Air. A friend from high school, Renee, who wanted to get out on her own, ended up as my roommate.

During this time I worked full-time at Hardee's in Churchville as the head grill man. Hardee's was my first real job and I was a quick study, excelling as the go-to guy. At not quite eighteen, I made enough of an impression that the regional manager came from North Carolina to meet me. He started grooming me for a management role. I still did a little bit of dealing on the side for a couple of dollars, but ultimately, I lived on legitimate work. Because I wasn't yet eighteen, I could not yet pursue management training, which annoyed me. Frustrated with not being old enough to move up, I lost patience with waiting and I went to Ocean City to seek a better job.

I took the Greyhound bus to the beach with a few dollars and no prospects in sight. My plan was to sleep under the boardwalk until I could get on my feet. Not the greatest idea in March. It was too cold. That first night I spent pretending to stay at the Quality Inn and found empty floors to sneak a catnap. The next morning I met a guy out on the boardwalk who told me about a woman who rented rooms for seasonal workers. He said she might let me stay rent-free until my first check. After he introduced me to her, she agreed to that arrangement. That same day I went job hunting and landed two restaurant jobs.

While I walked back along Coastal Highway from those interviews, a guy pulled over and offered me a ride. He asked if I was down for the summer for work and then proceeded to offer me a job working construction. His company was waterproofing the exterior of a condominium building. It paid a lot more than the restaurant jobs with a guaranteed ten hours of overtime per week. I took the offer and started working for them the next day. We worked on scaffolding on the outside of the building so I was working, getting paid, and getting a tan. It overwhelmed me financially because I still paid rent on my apartment in Abingdon on top of the additional rent in Ocean City. When the company found out about my living situation, they offered a spot at the condominium they rented to their work crew. For me, it was a total win and I was grateful for how everything seemed to be working out for me. After the beach job ended, the company asked me to stay with them in Baltimore. We worked jobs in the surrounding areas of Baltimore and Washington, DC.

Unfortunately, the reality of living on our own and dealing with bills caught up with Renee. Where I settled into the realities of working and supplementing my income to pay bills, Renee enjoyed the party scene and having her own place. After six months she decided to move back home. I kept the place until the end of summer. After my lease was up, I moved in with another friend named Billy. He also dealt cocaine, but a partner placed him in a bad situation and he wanted out. Within two months he decided to move to Texas and go back to school. He signed over his lease to me and I kept the apartment until the time of my arrest.

Around this time, I met up with an old friend who was looking to score some speed. Back then, stores sold speed look-alikes, in the form of caffeine and ephedrine pills. I purchased "speed" by the jarful. Then broke it down into packages of hundreds or thousands and resold them for big profits. I held a large network of customers that included bouncers, club owners, and bartenders. I could front product to them and realize high returns. Seeking even higher profits, I traded speed for cocaine. In the end, I sold cocaine exclusively. I was clueless at the time, but a childhood friend who went to college in Florida worked for the Medellin Cartel. He turned into my connection to a higher-quality product and distribution network. It propelled me from selling pieces of an ounce to selling weight (large quantities) to other dealers.

By May of 1981, dealing drugs emerged as my full-time occupation. While I knew how to work hard at a legitimate job, the lure of easy money and false prestige was too tempting for me. I got swept up in that lifestyle. In my personal reality, I was living the life. I planned to put aside my first million and return to school for a degree in restaurant management. I wanted to own and operate my own club in the long run. But something unexpected came along, and one phone call was the beginning of the end of this dream for me.

# CHAPTER 2

It was late Sunday afternoon, May 24, 1981, when Deno Kanaras, the cousin of a couple of my friends, called my apartment. His family owned a few local restaurants. He was a manager at one called the Fox's Den, located in downtown Bel Air. Kanaras wanted to buy an eight-ball of cocaine (an 8th of an ounce). I kept Kanaras at a distance because I didn't like or trust him. Once, he brought a couple of people to my place to buy cocaine. These were people I didn't know and bringing strangers to my apartment was something I didn't like. There was something shifty about Kanaras. He never looked anyone in the eyes and he lied a lot, even when there'd be no reason to. He inserted himself into the middle of drug deals trying to get "hit off," meaning treated to some cocaine by both buyer and dealer. This was a sort of custom, receiving a free, small amount of cocaine from a buyer or dealer (or both) after connecting the two for a deal. He was one of the few people I'd ever met that seemed addicted to cocaine. While far from the truth, cocaine wasn't considered an addictive drug by many at that time. It was a major reason cocaine became widely accepted in the higher levels of society during the eighties.

I was home alone expecting some product later in the evening. I told Kanaras he could check back. He was so anxious and pressing about it that I figured he'd find something somewhere else. Instead of calling back, he showed up at my apartment after several hours and wanted to wait. He seemed pretty keyed up and anxious. He said he snorted some crank, which I have never done, and he wanted to get some cocaine to balance out. I didn't want him to be there when my connection showed up, so when Kanaras suggested we go out and grab drinks I went along. We ended up at a local club outside of Bel Air called Pecora's, and hung out for a bit with the staff. Because it was a pretty slow Sunday, the owner said he was going to close. He suggested that Kanaras and I join him at another local club called the Golden 40. It sounded like a good idea and I told Kanaras that he should talk to Joe Hudson when we got there. Joe was a disc jockey at the Golden 40 and on several occasions, he sold my cocaine through the club. I thought he might have an 8-ball.

At the club, Joe & Kanaras negotiated a deal for an eight-ball, but it needed to wait until Joe got off work. When the bar closed, Kanaras and I followed Joe back to his house. He stayed in a camper parked at Long Bar Harbor, about fifteen miles east of Bel Air. Along the way, both cars stopped at a 7-11 store. Joe and I went inside for cigarettes. I found out through the trial that while we were inside, Kanaras got out of his car. He walked to the other vehicle to say hello to Joe's girlfriend, Diane. We arrived at the camper sometime after two o'clock in the morning. Kanaras and I waited in the car to give Joe and Diane time to pay their sitter and such. When Joe was ready, we went inside. We stayed long enough to conclude Kanaras' drug deal and for me and Joe to arrange a separate deal for another time. We left and Kanaras dropped me off at my apartment. I took a call from a good friend of mine who was having an all-night house party. It was close to three o'clock in the morning by then. Tired and uninterested in going back out, I declined and went to bed.

Late Monday morning, I woke up to a call from Kanaras. He seemed agitated and weird saying he needed to talk to me and he was coming over. He showed up very withdrawn and spaced out. Eyes wired, he still wore the same clothes from the night before. He told me he got into some shit and needed me to say we were together all night if anyone asked. I planned to go see some friends at the weekend-long Fiddler's Convention. This was a bluegrass festival held at Susquehanna State Park in Cecil County. I said we should go there as I couldn't imagine anyone believing that I would let Kanaras stay at my place. Everyone knew I didn't care for him. On the way to the festival, we dropped by my parent's house in Churchville. My mother asked me to speak to my brother, who declared he wanted to quit high school. She asked if I would do it before she and my father left for their vacation. I spent at least thirty minutes inside the house while Kanaras sat in his car. We made another quick stop at my friend Tom Hall's house, about three houses down from my parents. I made plans to meet Tom that afternoon to borrow his car, then Kanaras drove us out to Cecil County. We stayed at the Fiddler's Convention for an hour before Kanaras drove me to Hall's Furniture store to grab the car I arranged to borrow. We parted ways and I drove to Pimlico Race Track in Baltimore City. I met up with my friend, Tommy Dellis, who happens to be another of Kanaras' cousins.

I never gave the alibi request another thought throughout the day. I didn't mention it to Dellis either. That night I went to my girlfriend's house where I got a call from Kanaras' other cousin, Tommy Kanaras. Tommy said the police contacted him and wanted to speak to me about Deno. He asked me what his cousin got himself into. I told him I didn't know but thought, I should go talk to the cops. I did not want my girlfriend involved in any of this and Tommy agreed to come by and pick me up when he got off work. I wasn't giving much thought to what I was getting into. My controlling thoughts were to make my statement and put this behind me. In hindsight that was a little more than naive. If I understood what was going on I would have exercised more common sense and not gotten involved.

Around midnight, Tuesday, May 26th, Tommy dropped me off at the Harford County sheriff's office, located in downtown Bel Air and I knocked on their door. When I told them my name and said that I heard they wanted to talk to me, they whisked me into a small interrogation room in the back. Sergeant VanHorn interviewed me. At first, the questions were benign. Was I with Kanaras last night? What did we do? Where did we go? I kept to the script and provided them the alibi Kanaras asked me for.

At that point, the tone changed and they called me a liar. They knew better and out of nowhere, I heard I was being investigated for a double murder. I didn't know what to do, what to say. I thought, what the hell is going on and how do I get out of this mess? I told them I didn't know anything about any murders and I wasn't part of anything like that. I volunteered to take a lie detector test. Then I told them they could search me, my apartment, whatever they wanted. The sergeant seized on my offer to search my apartment and asked if I would give consent. They jumped on my brief hesitation, asking me, "What are we going to find?" In that instant, I knew my drug dealing days were over. I admitted to them that I possessed drug paraphernalia and it was in my apartment. The cops asked if I was willing to turn that stuff in. As of that moment, I retired from that life forever and I said yes.

Police escorted me to my apartment and conducted their search. I turned in my triple beam and quad scales along with other assorted drug paraphernalia. They were very interested in having me take the lie detector test. I said I would contact a lawyer and have it set up. For the moment satisfied, they left for the night. During the night and in the early morning, Kanaras tried to call me a couple of times. I ignored him. I was furious at him for getting me involved but scared to talk to him. Kanaras comes from a large extended family. Town talk led me to believe they were part of something much like La Cosa Nostra. Kanaras' older cousin, someone I looked up to, alluded they were a part of something bigger, calling it the Sons of Pericles. I didn't know what was going on with the police investigation, but I didn't want any part of it. But I lived by a code of honor. My word is my bond and I don't break it. I committed to providing this alibi. Taking the lie detector test was the most reasonable thing that came to mind in order to prove that I wasn't involved. All I wanted was to extricate myself from this.

When the cops left my apartment I noticed a couple of missed calls on my answering machine. They were from Kanaras. I was in no mood to talk to him so I didn't bother to return the calls. He called back the next morning which I ignored once more. Tommy Kanaras drove away the night before when I didn't come back out of the sheriff's office. I would never see or speak to him again. I assume that he told Kanaras that he waited for me in the parking lot and I never returned. Not knowing if I covered his alibi might have sent Kanaras into a panic. Or, since he couldn't reach me, maybe he thought I got arrested. When couldn't reach me, Kanaras got a lawyer and turned himself in. He concocted the story that I held him hostage while I committed the crimes.

That morning I called my sister Pam for help. I didn't have a lawyer or know one. I remembered the father of a friend from high school was an attorney. I looked in the phone book for Getz and Getz. The address happened to be across from the Harford County Sheriff's Station. My sister's boyfriend took me to the law firm and we ended up parking in the lot behind the Sheriff's Station.

I walked into that law firm without an appointment or anything. I said, "I'm here to see Mr. Getz." It turned out that my friend's father was a civil attorney. But, his uncle was a criminal attorney in the same practice, so I met with him. It was a straightforward meeting. I described what happened the night before and told him I volunteered to take a lie detector test. I wanted his help to set it up. He agreed to assist me and contact the sheriff's department to set up a lie detector test. I felt more confident because I knew that when I passed this test I'd be out of this mess. I left Mr. Getz's office, relieved that there was a good plan.

As my sister's boyfriend and I walked back to the car, we passed by the restaurant owned by Kanaras' father and uncles. Mr. Kanaras happened to be standing outside smoking a cigarette. We exchanged greetings, nothing more. What I hadn't noticed while getting into the car was that Mr. Kanaras turned on his heel and strode right inside the station. As we pulled out, I saw the back door of the station open. Officers ran out with guns drawn. I told my sister's boyfriend to stop because there was no one else in the parking lot. I sensed they were coming for me. Sure enough, they surrounded us, shouting, "Get out of the car, hands up!" That was the last time my feet hit the free pavement for thirty-two years, two months, and twenty-eight days.

That was the beginning of my whole nightmare journey.

# CHAPTER 3

Joseph I. Cassilly was an Assistant State's Attorney in Harford County in 1981. He served in that role for the County State's Attorneys' Office for a period of five years, starting in 1977. While serving in the army, he suffered a serious injury that left him wheelchair-bound. I did not know him, but our mothers were acquaintances as our sisters took piano lessons from the same instructor. I based my initial impression of him on the relationship between our mothers. I felt he was doing his job and would be open to the truth. Cassilly would go on to exploit that naivety and betray my trust in the system. After my second trial in 1983, he ran for and won the election to become the State's Attorney for Harford County. He saw reelection to this position eight times over 36 years, making him the longest serving state's prosecutor in Maryland.

His office charged me with the brutal stabbing death of Diane Becker and the shooting death of Joseph "Joe" Hudson. A drug-related, double homicide the papers dubbed as the Memorial Day Murders. All because I agreed to Kanaras' request for help with an alibi. I involved myself in the drug world and immersed myself in that lifestyle. I was young, anti-police, anti-establishment, things like that. I didn't think twice about giving Kanaras an alibi. I was like, "No problem." My reward for helping him was that he turned himself in through his parents' high-powered attorneys. On May 27, 1981, Kanaras gave a formal statement to the Harford County Sheriff's Office that claimed I committed these horrific crimes and held him, hostage, while doing so. In June, 1981, he testified before a grand jury which led to my indictment.

It took about six months for this to go to trial. During this time I remained incarcerated at Harford County Detention Center. My charges included two counts of premeditated murder and two counts of first-degree felony murder. After my arrest, I went before the judge for a bail hearing. The judge denied bail and I remained incarcerated. Kanaras was also arrested, but given bail of one hundred thousand dollars. He posted it and gained his release from custody. A few weeks later Kanaras caught a separate charge. This one was for a drug deal he brokered that involved undercover police. Because it was an active investigation, they did not arrest Kanaras at the time of the sale. Instead, a judge sealed an indictment against him while the undercover operation continued. Authorities wanted to see if they could net others up the chain. The way I saw it, Kanaras wanted to totally get himself out of the murder charges. He knew about a shipment coming in via Texas, a lot of cocaine, and he gave the cops what information he knew. They were able to bust the transporter, a guy named John Haas. John was a local bouncer. He worked at Pecora's and at another bar, but was hired mainly to run the drugs up from Texas to Maryland. Hass got busted in the parking lot of what used to be Golden Ring Mall, just north of Baltimore City, with several hundred thousand dollars worth of coke. When the operation ended they arrested him on drug charges. At yet another bail review, the court granted it. This time it totaled thirty-five thousand dollars. He posted it and got released, without spending any time in jail. Between these bail hearings, Kanaras provided information that led to the confiscation of cocaine and the arrest and conviction of several other individuals. When he no longer possessed any useful information, the State petitioned the court to revoke both of his bails, stating he was a flight risk. They took Kanaras into custody and placed him in the same detention center where I was awaiting my trial.

The detention center kept us apart under what is called an enemy alert. We were housed in separate areas while there. When I received visitors, I ended up on the women's side. They never let us be in the hallway at the same time or in the visiting room at the same time. In the visiting room, you stood and looked through a little plate glass that's maybe four inches by twelve inches. Inmates used a phone when speaking to their visitors. On the men's side, you just walked down the hallway and got on the phone. I had to go over to the women's side because there was a door that could lock. I was locked into the women's area during my visits.

By the time my trial took place in November 1981, the attention in the media and from the prosecution focused on me. Kanaras admitted he was present at the scene during the murders and subsequent robberies. He insisted that I was the trigger man who held him, hostage, fearing for his life, throughout the ordeal. Hairs taken from the clothing and bedspread of one of the victims were allegedly mine. My fingerprint was allegedly found on a glass vodka bottle claimed to be a murder weapon. Multiple "experts" took the stand and it seemed like a slam dunk for the prosecution. But I was young and naive enough to assume it would straighten itself out in court for the simple reason that I didn't do it.

There was an automatic change of venue because the state sought the death penalty. My trial moved to the rural country town of Denton, located in Caroline County, Maryland. A town even smaller than my own hometown of Churchville. Everyone knew everyone in Denton. At the first trial, I could not afford to hire a private attorney. This meant the public defender's office represented me. They assigned Stephen Tarrant as my attorney. His slight stutter sometimes interfered with how he presented our defense to the jury. Still, Tarrant did the best he could and presented five days of solid defense.

Cassilly gave the opening statement for the state. Their theory was that I killed Joe out of a desperate need for money. Further, they suggested I murdered Diane because she could identify me and Kanaras. The prosecution claimed that I had both opportunity and ability to commit the crime. Cassilly told the jury he could show, beyond a reasonable doubt, what happened between 2:00 a.m. and 10:00 a.m. on Sunday, May 25, 1981. The defense deferred our opening statement and the state called its witnesses.

Tina Weidener, a teenager who babysat for Joe and Diane the night they were killed, was among the first to testify. On the stand, she told the court that Diane returned to the trailer the morning of May 25th around 1:30 a.m. with a man named David Britton. She watched as Diane dealt him some coke, taking it out of a box from the cabinet above the refrigerator. Next to the box were rolls of cash. Weidener witnessed the exchange of cash for cocaine between Diane and Britton. The two of them stayed about fifteen minutes, then left together to go back to Club 40. Weidnener also stated that this wasn't the first time Britton was at the trailer. According to her testimony, Britton visited the trailer a week before on a night Joe was at work. He stayed about a half hour. When he left, Weidnener went to see Diane who told her she dealt him some cocaine. To my knowledge, Britton was barely interviewed by the police, even though he was alone with Diane one week, and then just hours, before her murder. His signed statement and testimony during my trial were used to corroborate the babysitter's testimony about the presence of drugs and cash in the trailer. From there, the prosecution moved on to other witnesses and then, Kanaras.

Now, by calling a witness an attorney attests to that witness's honesty and veracity. No attorney may present any witness who they know is not telling the truth. One big key to the prosecution's case was the testimony from Kanaras. His was the singular narrative presented. The problem was that the prosecution's team did not trust him. They said that "...expert witnesses and the prosecution don't consider Kanaras' version of events credible." There were "too many inconsistencies...between certain [parts] of the physical evidence." In fact, the prosecution was unable to present him as a State witness against me. They petitioned the court to call Kanaras as a Court witness. I also learned the state gave Kanaras two lie detector tests, both of which he failed. This was another reason why the prosecutor was unable to present him as a witness. The state prosecuted him on the same murder charges in a trial that occurred after mine. Thus, Kanaras could not claim that he was a state's witness at my trial and therefore receive any validation for his testimony. The judge granted the petition and the prosecution called Kanaras as a court witness during my first trial.

The hardest thing in the world was to sit in silence and listen to someone tell blatant lies without responding. Kanaras spent hours on the witness stand spinning a bizarre and unrealistic account of this crime with the blame targeted at me. It seemed like a very rehearsed spiel, almost as if he was reading from a script. The cross-examination revealed the discrepancies and inconsistencies in his story. Kanaras became flustered and angry, and stumbled over his responses. He was inconsistent with certain details. In particular, Kanaras wanted to paint the picture that the gun used to murder Joe Hudson was mine. While he admitted buying it from a customer while working in the restaurant, he claimed he got rid of it a week later when his father found out. But his stories failed to add up.

In his formal police statement, taken two days after the murders, Kanaras informed the deputies that he purchased the gun one month prior to the murders. Then traded it to me for cocaine one week before the murders. In his grand jury testimony, Kanaras said he purchased the gun four to five months before the murders (January/February 1981) but sold it to me two to three months afterward (March/April 1981). Then in my trial, he testified that he purchased the gun one to two months before the murders (March/April 1981). But he caught himself because his testimony needed to match another witness who claimed she saw the gun at my apartment in February '81. Kanaras backtracked, "No, I purchased it two to three months before the murders, had it for a week, then sold it John." (February/March 1981). It's head spinning! When the defense pointed out that his three sets of testimony about the gun all differed, Kanaras replied, "I was never clear about the whole matter to begin with [pause] the time frame."

He also made contrary statements related to cleaning his car the day after the murders. On the stand during my trial, he told the court he, "...wiped down the front seat." Yet, in a statement to the sheriff's office two days after the crimes, Kanaras told them, "I wiped down the seats with a wet rag and vacuumed the interior." He was adamant during my trial that I never told him how much money I allegedly took from the Hudson mobile home. But, in his grand jury testimony Kanaras told the court in detail that while at my apartment after the murders, I took the money out of my pocket, counted it, and told him it was about $2,300.00. One might think by November of '81 his stories would match, especially since my trial was the third time he recalled them for officials. I remained quiet throughout and tried to maintain my composure. My attorneys warned me not to show emotions as the jury watched for any reactions.

In the middle of Kanaras' testimony, my concern surfaced when a woman walked right up to the jury box and passed a note to one of the male jurors. The judge seized the note and ordered deputies to detain the woman. The judge called her and Juror #6 to the bench. He asked her what she was doing and what the note meant. On the note was one word: soybeans. It turned out Juror #6 was this woman's husband. He explained to the court, "I guess the man has come to combine our soybeans." His wife confirmed it and urged her husband to come home as soon as possible when court ended. It was a surreal moment and not the best sign of how this jury would untangle a high-level drug and murder case. It was clear to me there was a sense of urgency to wrap up the trial, as there were other priorities for the community.

Kanaras continued for days to insist he feared for his life, he didn't know what to do, that I forced him to commit robbery. Every other word he used described himself as "terrified," "shocked," or in "a state of shock." Kanaras' story from the start was implausible. My attorney did a good job exposing many of the holes in his description of events. Tarrant pointed out that on one hand, Kanaras was fearful for his life after he claimed he saw me murder two people. But on the other hand, he at no time tried to overpower me or get away despite his stories supporting multiple occasions where he could have fled. Tarrant also pointed out another serious flaw in Kanaras' claim that I was armed. Somehow, through a night of driving around together, bar hopping, drinking, and doing lines of coke, he claimed I was able to conceal a gun, a knife, and a box of shells on my person. Kanaras' story continued to minimize his involvement with each new version.

The state's case against me included testimony from three FBI agents presumed to be experts in their field. This included the testimony of former FBI agent Michael Malone, who the state presented as an expert in fiber and hair examination at the time. It was his job to determine if fibers or hair came from a particular item or person. He claimed that two of my head hairs were found on items taken from the crime scene. Using a technique called microscopic hair analysis, he testified that the hairs found on items belonging to Diane Becker microscopically matched my head hairs. Malone claimed that in a side-by-side comparison, where he looked for 15 individual characteristics to compare, the questioned hairs were indistinguishable from mine, "[He] could not tell them apart." He ruled out the known hair samples from Kanaras and Joe Hudson, but not Diane Becker. Malone admitted that he failed to rule her out as a potential source and he admitted the science could not determine whether the hairs in question were male versus female. When pressed by my attorney about fiber comparison, Malone admitted he received my boots but did not attempt to match my boot fibers to any fibers found on the items given to him to process for evidence.

Another FBI agent, Donald Havekost, used a procedure called Comparative Lead Bullet Analysis (CLBA). He linked bullets recovered from the victim's body to live rounds found in the gun and to bullets recovered from different locations that Kanaras took investigators to. Havekost agreed with Cassilly that, "...the chances of our recovering bullets in three different locations in this case..which all have the same lead compositional content..." as the live rounds found in the gun, was a "...fairly significant find." Havekost's testimony provided no direct link between the bullets or the gun in this case to me. The prosecution went solely on the word of Kanaras.

The last FBI agent claimed that rifling tests proved the bullets recovered from the victim's body matched the barrel of the pistol identified as the murder weapon. Still, he was unable to link the gun or bullets to me.

Back then, there wasn't any science to dispute these tests or the "experts" who used them. All three FBI agents would have their testimony challenged decades later and/or the science they based their testimony on called into question.

The state presented other circumstantial evidence, such as my fingerprint on a vodka bottle. It was allegedly used as a murder weapon to inflict blunt force trauma to the back of Diane's head. I never tried to provide any concocted story about how my print appeared on the bottle. If I moved that bottle at any point during my time at the trailer, then of course it's conceivable that I left a print. The prosecution argued that my fingerprint was present after utilizing it as a murder weapon, but could not prove the exact time I left my print on the bottle. What the state over-looked and minimized was that there were over twenty other unidentified prints on that bottle. None of those were ever pur-sued. There was also a pair of pants Kanaras claimed were mine, found bleached, which he said was an attempt to remove blood.

When it was time for the defense to present my case, we questioned witnesses that rebutted previous testimony and the version of events Kanaras clung to. One important witness, a jail-house inmate named Anthony Williams, testified that he asked Kanaras if John committed the murders and Kanaras told him, "No." Williams also asked Kanaras about the pants. Kanaras told him they weren't mine but did not ever say who they belonged to. Since Kanaras told Williams that I didn't commit the murders, Williams assumed Kanaras did it. He asked him why he shot Joe so many times. In his testimony, Williams told the court that Kanaras said, "If he had used more wide cutters, that he wouldn't have to shoot him so many times."

It took two weeks of testimony before the jury was to rule. They deliberated my fate for two days before they rendered a verdict. As I stood to hear the reading of the verdict, I felt non-plussed as I waited for justice. I dealt with a myriad of emotions and, quite frankly, I lacked the coping skills to deal with them all. I held on to a very misguided sense that the truth would set me free. Two solid weeks of eight-hour days in the courtroom where I felt helpless compounded my anxiety. My trial dehumanized and demonized me to the point my personality no longer existed. I was sub-human, an object. It made me numb. The judge read off the verdict and I received the justice I deserved, Not Guilty of premeditated murder. It was over. My emotions were soaring. Every part of me felt a rush of relief. But in a nanosecond, that feeling came crashing down. The prosecution also charged me with first-degree felony murder in the same count of the indictment. The judge read, "Guilty." I didn't understand what happened. In an instant, I went from elation and relief to fear and anxiety. I was so shocked, that my legs buckled beneath me. Court officers whisked me out of the courtroom before I could speak with my attorney. I returned to the Harford County detention center and awaited the sentencing proceeding.

Within a month I went back to court to learn my fate. Not much to say at that point. A few people came as character witnesses, but not many. The problem with involving myself in the drug world meant most of my current friends lived the same lifestyle. They didn't want to be near a courtroom. The light flicked on and like cockroaches, my so-called friends scurried to hide. The police put a lot of pressure on my girlfriend at the time, Kim. They pestered her at work trying to get her to say anything incriminating. We would never speak again after my arrest because it was too much for her. That same over-the-top police pressure was happening to many of my friends who had been listed as possible character witnesses. This included my Juvenile Probation Officer who was berated by the Harford

County Sheriff's investigators for his willingness to provide testimony for me.

My mother was in the courtroom. Mom was very loyal like that. She maintained faith in my innocence the whole way. When the judge pronounced the sentence, two death penalties plus twenty-one years, I turned to check on her. She was in tears. I felt crushed and helpless. Even though it was difficult to stand, I tried to comfort her with a smile. I couldn't hug her, or say a single word, before guards escorted out and took me straight to the penitentiary.

# CHAPTER 4

Prison is a different world with its own rules and codes, making it hard to adjust. These are men convicted of serious crimes of violence. At worst, I was a drug dealer. There's nothing to prepare a person for life inside. When I first arrived, I wasn't the happiest camper with two death penalties hanging over me. The warden had two rules: 1) don't jump on my officers and 2) don't jump on my walls. Other than that, anything else went. Once I came around a corner, and a guy was getting stabbed to death in a blind spot right in front of the laundry room. I turned on my heels and went back the other way. I thought *they're going to lock it down and it's going to get worse in here*. I was wrong. They sprinkled sand over the blood and the penitentiary operated like normal. That was the value of life inside those walls. It was non-existent.

Most of my first year inside I spent hitting the law library. Although meager, there were issues of *Georgetown Law Journal*, access to old law books, and donated materials. This was before any access to on line systems to order case law through the library.

I immersed myself in fighting for my freedom. I started writing motions based on case law. Despite my focus on learning case law and penning arguments, there was that other side of me. My anger and frustration at the situation bubbled under the surface. It was hard to contain but I stayed out of trouble and put that energy into my case. Meanwhile, Kanaras went on trial in March 1982.

During his trial testimony, Kanaras continued to claim that while he was present during the murders, I coerced him, he was in fear of me, and innocent of committing the crimes. The state did not believe him and laid their case before his jury. Among the many lies and inconsistencies in his accounting was that he first denied ever being at the mobile home where Diane's murder occurred. He later changed that story to yet another lie; he was there, but nothing happened. When questioned at his home, if he was with anyone at any time during the night before. He said, "John," but claimed he didn't know the last name. Kanaras' mother insisted they could make a call to find out "John's" last name. When the cops contacted his cousin, Tommy, they figured out Kanaras was referring to me. It was after Tommy dropped me off at the station that Kanaras fabricated his story.

The state went on in Kanaras' trial to illuminate the inconsistencies and lies riddled throughout his statements to the police and the grand jury. For example, he claimed that I carried the murder weapon in my boot after the murder of Diane Becker; however, it wasn't the inside of my boot where the investigators found traces of human blood. It was Kanaras'.

The state presented several witnesses who refuted Kanaras' testimony. The most striking was Steve Rassa. During pre-trial objections and issues, the state brought up issues over Rassa's safety, fearing physical harm. Cassilly described Rassa as "...very uneasy and uncomfortable in cooperating with the State." He felt intimidated by and was afraid of the Kanaras family. Cassilly illustrated this when he went on to say, "He [Rassa] was at one time a friend of the defendant. He was concerned that the defendant's relatives or someone may try to intimidate him." Rassa was insistent that he did not want to testify. The judge ruled that without basis or proof of danger, Rassa would have to appear in court.

Once on the stand, Rassa testified that on May 20, 1981, five days before the crimes occurred, he was with Kanaras as he tried at three different locations to sell several gold chains and a gold and diamond ring given to Kanaras by his father. At the first location, Rassa said that Kanaras went in and came right back out - someone there spooked him. Rassa testified that,

> *"Something had scared Deno about Mr. Soltis, and when I went out to Deno and asked him what was strong, he said that Mr. Soltis was a good friend of his father's and he didn't want his father to know anything about him selling the jewelry."*

Rassa goes on to say that they had no luck selling any of the gold chains at any of the locations; however, at the third business, the buyer asked about the gold and diamond ring Kanaras wore. Rassa talked him out of selling it citing sentimental value. Leaving the jeweler, Rassa asked, "Don't you feel a lot better that you didn't sell your jewelry?" Kanaras agreed and stated he knew someone that he might be able to borrow a couple of thousand dollars. In Kanaras' account for enforcement, he portrayed himself as a successful businessman with no pressing debt or need for money. Yet, five days before the murders he was trying to sell his jewelry without his dad finding out and mentioned his need to "borrow a couple of thousand dollars."

According to Rassa's testimony, they gave up trying to sell the jewelry. Instead, they went back to Edgewood and bought a gram of crank (methamphetamine). They each did some of the crank, smoked a joint, and tried to sell the leftover meth with no luck. Later they ended up at Hudson's trailer at Long Bar Harbor. Rassa testified that as they pulled up outside the trailer, Kanaras reached under Rassa's seat. In Rassa's testimony, he asked Kanaras,

"*What are you doing?* Kanaras replied *I'm getting my gun*. And I said, *Leave it there. Don't get your gun. I don't want any parts of anything like this.* I wasn't sure what was going to happen, so I said let's go in. Kanaras reached under the seat a second time, and I said, *What are you doing?* Kanaras says, *Getting my gun. I want to show it to you.* And I said, Deno, *I don't need to see your gun, I've seen it before. Just leave it there.* Then I asked him, *Is there*

*something you're not telling me? Do you owe Joe money?*
And there was no reply."

Rassa continued on the stand to say he asked Kanaras if he thought that he could get away with robbing and shooting someone in the middle of a trailer park in broad daylight. Kanaras' response was, "I have a knife in the glove compartment." Rassa in turn responded by asking Kanaras if he thought he could stab someone with a knife, to which Kanaras said, "No, but you could."

Although Rassa claimed he wanted nothing to do with any part of robbing Joe Hudson, both ended up inside Hudson's trailer to buy cocaine. Rassa says they hung out with Diane for about ten minutes before Joe returned and Kanaras' demeanor made Rassa very nervous the entire time. He testified that after three tries he convinced Kanaras to sit down. Rassa remained uneasy, still unsure about what might happen. It was getting dark and Rassa told the court, "I remembered that I didn't want to be in that trailer after dark." When Joe arrived, all four did a line or two of cocaine. Then Rassa told Joe that Kanaras wanted to make a purchase. The fee was $45 for half a gram. Kanaras paid Joe twenty-five dollars and told him that he would be at the Golden 40 later that evening to pay the rest. Joe asked Kanaras, "What about the other money?" Rassa said he went to the restroom at this point and while he could tell Joe and Kanaras were having a conversation, he could not make out what they said.

During the defense cross-examination, the prosecution informed the judge that while on a brief recess, "...one of the Kanaras people came up to him [Rassa] and said words like, "You still have problems fella?" This made the prosecution somewhat concerned for Rassa's safety, making it the second time they brought this issue up to the court. The judge noted that others in the courtroom also claimed they observed activity from the Kanaras gallery that seemed like an attempt to "...have [an] impact or exert influence on people who are called to testify, regardless of who they are." The judge ordered the defense to instruct the Kanaras group to sit straight-faced and observe in silence.

Another witness, Tommy Wagner, testified that he saw the gun, held it, and examined it in April 1981. He said Kanaras tried to sell it to him for $150, but at the time Wagner couldn't afford it. Prior to the trial, he saw an array of guns shown to him by the prosecution. They asked him to choose the one belonging to Kanaras. Wagner picked out the gun identified as the murder weapon by an animal carved in the handgrip. His testimony contradicted the defense witness who claimed she saw it in my possession at my apartment in February '81. Wagner was later charged with and served time for selling cocaine to the undercover troopers in drug deals that Kanaras set up. I never met Tommy Wagner but knew who he was. I met his roommate and was aware that they lived in a different section of the same apartment complex as mine.

A third witness placed the gun in Kanaras' possession. He was a former undercover state police trooper, Aschenbach. The trooper testified in the Kanaras trial that while undercover on March 25, 1981, Kanaras set up a deal where the trooper purchased $2000 worth of cocaine. Before he and Kanaras left, Kanaras went to his car, which was parked head-on in front of the trooper's unmarked car. The trooper witnessed Kanaras reach under the front driver's seat and place something in his pocket. Returning to the trooper's car, Kanaras remarked that he never went on [drug] deals involving this much money without his "piece." The trooper explained to the court that "piece" meant a weapon, most often, a handgun. Kanaras denied this and claimed the gun was at his home on March 25, 1981, not in his car - in direct conflict with his testimony in my trial where he claimed he sold it to me in February/March 1981. The trooper's testimony includes that on two separate occasions Kanaras set up a deal between the trooper and a drug dealer. One of those occasions was March 25, 1981, and the other was on February 3, 1981. After each deal, the trooper allowed Kanaras a small taste of the cocaine that was acquired. Aschenbach explained:

*"It is customary in the drug culture for a person introducing another person, or a third party, for the purpose [of] purchasing drugs, often they expect some sort of payment and in many cases that payment is often expected in part of the drug that is purchased."*

Furthermore, the trooper testified to various conversations and encounters where Kanaras demonstrated a very clear and pressing need for money. He testified that Kanaras concocted a scheme to attach some kind of wire to his nightly bank deposit, allowing him to pull it back out of the machine. The trooper also enticed Kanaras with a fictitious story about a friend who wanted to hire someone to blow up his boat in order to collect $20K in insurance money.

My father, who was not called as a witness during my first trial, contradicted Kanaras' hostage claim and alleged duress. After I accompanied Kanaras to establish an alibi, we stopped by my parents' house. While I was inside for about half an hour, Kanaras remained in the car in the driveway. I wasn't aware during my first trial that my father spoke with Kanaras while I was inside, much less that my father was a witness to anything. He detailed Kanaras' calm demeanor and chatty nature.

Rassa's testimony highlighted Kanaras' need for money. It clearly established that there were previous drug transactions between Joe and Kanaras. Deals for which Kanaras still owed Joe money. Not to mention, it placed the gun and the knife in Kanaras' possession five days before the murders. Aschenbach and Wagner testified that Kanaras owned the gun in April and March of 1981, despite his claim that he sold it to me for cocaine in February of 1981. According to Aschenbach, Kanaras also exploited an established tradition of serving as a sort of broker to gain free product, which highlighted Kanaras' addiction and cunning.

The worst part was that my defense team knew nothing about these exculpatory witnesses. That is until we read about them in the local paper covering the trial. Throughout his various testimonies, Kanaras shifted the blame to me. He presented himself as a successful business owner who didn't need to commit a crime involving money or drugs. These witnesses contradicted Kanaras' claims of not owning the weapons as well as claims of personal success and wealth. Since they were unknown to us at my trial, my jury didn't hear any of this testimony. They heard Kanaras' testimony without contradiction. It was a clear violation of the Brady rule. The rule requires that the prosecution must turn over all exculpatory evidence to the defendant in a criminal case.

After learning of these witnesses, my lawyer filed a Brady Motion claiming a violation of the discovery requirements by the state's attorney. Because I was on appeal, the judge held that motion but never ruled on it because the Court of Appeals awarded me a new trial based on the improper rebuttal evidence presented by the state. In the appeal process, my attorneys requested a retrial as there was testimony from Kim, my girlfriend at the time, presented as rebuttal after the defense rested their case. She testified that we talked about taking a trip to Florida together, which we did; but, the State framed her statements as showing I planned to flee. My defense did not have the chance to cross-examine this witness and requested a new trial based on improper rebuttal testimony. During my testimony at the trial I was not asked about any trip to Florida. Therefore, the state's attorney presented inappropriate testimony as it rebutted nothing. In fact, Kim testified she, "...talked to the Sheriff's office six times, and I felt pressured. I have talked to so many people and said so many things that I am totally confused." It was a maneuver by the prosecution to present her testimony as a final influence on the jury without the means for my legal team to dispute it.

Locked in my cell on death row a year later almost to the day, I turned on the evening news. I saw a promo for an upcoming news story about an inmate granted a new trial in a death penalty case. The story ended up being about me, although I couldn't concentrate after hearing my name. The Court of Appeals granted me a new trial by a 5/4 vote. I felt relieved! The court gave me the chance to correct this wrong. The time it took to make this decision seemed excessive to me, but I guessed the universe meant it to happen this way. I felt that my innocence manifested this path toward redemption and the truth.

# CHAPTER 5

For the new trial, the court system transferred me back out to Harford County Detention Center. I sat for about a year waiting on my second trial date. Being in a detention center was a lot harder to deal with after having been in the penitentiary. Detention centers are more confined than the Pen. The guards and staff in the penitentiary will give the inmates more respect because they're right there with them, as compared to Harford County deputies who work the jail but yearn to be regular police. I started getting into a little jailhouse-type trouble. There were some run-ins with officers and guards because I don't like people to put their hands on me in an aggressive way. I ended up getting street charges that were thrown out, except for one charge for an attempted escape for which I got sentenced to five years. Cassilly also visited me in jail prior to my second trial, in violation of every single attorney's ethic and code of conduct. My attorney was not present or notified of his intent to call on me. He offered me a plea bargain, but when challenged in court by my attorney, Cassilly denied the conversation. He couldn't hide the fact he made the visit because jail records documented it. He offered the flimsy excuse that he was unable to reach my new attorney and was checking in with me to see if I was happy with my representation.

At my first trial, the jury found me not guilty of two counts of first-degree premeditated murder. However, they found me guilty of two counts of first-degree felony murder in the same count. I never wrapped my head around that. The statutory law allows for this to occur, but I could not let it go. From my cell, I wrote a sixty-page motion citing double jeopardy and requested to have the case thrown out. I was learning the law as I was writing the motion. In my research, I came across a principle of law called *collateral estoppel*. This stated that facts already ruled on cannot be relitigated. In my view, the charges in the second trial were the same as in the first trial. I felt it was illegal under this law. We argued the motion in the Court of Appeals the weekend before the trial started and the court denied it. Expecting to win that motion I left the trial preparations to my new, court-appointed attorney, Alan Drew. All of the transcripts and the investigation from the first trial were in his possession for reference. Plus, there was more at that point because Kanaras went to trial after me.

In my first trial, our defense lasted five eight-hour days. With the addition of these new witnesses, I expected a very robust defense. However, my attorney, Alan Drew, waited until the weekend in the middle of the trial to hire an investigator. The prosecution once more presented and rested their case. We had the weekend to button up ours. This time the trial was in

Frederick County, where I sat in their county jail. Drew sent an investigator to meet with me on Saturday, the weekend before we were to present our case. He asked, "Well, who do you want me to subpoena?"

With my case slated to present evidence on Monday, this confused and astounded me. How was that going to work? At the very start of Drew's assignment to my case, I gave him the list of witnesses used at the first trial and included the additional witnesses we learned about from Kanaras' trial. It was shocking that Drew hadn't already subpoenaed them and that he waited until now before he brought on an investigator for the case. It was no surprise the investigator ran into trouble locating witnesses at the eleventh hour. I doubt there was much effort expended finding them. Monday morning came and Drew announced to me that we weren't presenting a defense. He tried to sell me on this as a tactical decision since he felt the prosecution's case was weak. In reality, he didn't present a defense because he didn't have any witnesses and wasn't prepared. After the state rested, we rested.

What was I to do? I didn't get the chance to testify on my own behalf. Going to court from within the prison system is already hard enough because of the extra toll it exacts. Transportation came for me so early, it meant I missed breakfast. I sat in holding cells alone, with no external stimuli. Lunch consisted of a bologna and cheese sandwich which I ate again for dinner due to late nights at the courthouse. Sleep-deprived with wash-ups in a sink because I missed the shower schedule. Day after day of this. My mental state was off balance and it affected my ability to absorb information and make prudent decisions.

The second trial resulted in a reconviction, sentenced to death, and sent back to the penitentiary. Once more, guards escorted me behind those miserable walls of granite and into the land of hate and despair.

# CHAPTER 6

The first few months incarcerated, awaiting the first trial, went by without any trouble between me and the staff or fellow inmates. I was misunderstood and placed my confidence in a system that didn't exist. I was more overwhelmed, anxious, and stressed than angry. After the outcome of the second trial, I found myself angry and frustrated. In my mind's eye, the system failed me yet again. Making it worse, the court-appointed attorney royally screwed me over. Nothing was in my control and I no longer believed the system worked.

When the jury rendered their guilty verdict the second time, it took two months before I went back for sentencing. That's when I decided I didn't need to hang around to go back to death row. I smuggled hacksaw blades into the detention center and went to work on the bars separating our tier from the guard walkway. I heard rumors that the bars in the detention center were roller bars, meaning that inside the bar casing was a round rod that would roll if exposed, not letting a blade bite into it. For that reason, I sawed the frame that held the bars instead. It took more than a week to get almost the whole way through the frame. Then the last 1/32" of an inch wouldn't cut through. I placed it on hold and smuggled in new blades, this time diamond crusted hacksaw blades. These worked like a charm and made the final cuts. I slid through my opening onto the guard tier with the one thing between me and freedom being a louvered window. I pulled the heavy-duty screen from its frame and tried sawing the hinge of one of the louver windows. For my collective efforts, and a brand new diamond blade I saved up for that part, I was unable to cut that hinge. I tried for a good twenty minutes before acknowledging defeat and climbing back into the housing unit. I broke my blades into little pieces, flushed them down the toilet, and lay on my bunk for lock-in and count. I expected the guard to notice the screen hanging from its frame or the cut bars, but he walked the length of the tier, made his headcount, and left without seeing any of it.

I woke from sleep in the wee hours of the morning to spotlights shining through the windows and helicopter blades whirling. The officers banged on our doors and shouted for us to report to the dayroom. At first, they thought someone climbed up on the roof to break in but they soon figured it out. Of course, officials sought the help of the usual jailhouse snitches and they recovered my fingerprints from the outside glass of the window. It was enough for their case. I didn't deny it. With two death penalties plus twenty-one extra years, I decided I didn't care anymore. That got me an additional five-year sentence and immortalization at the Harford County Detention Center. From that point on the guards did a bar check on their rounds, hitting the bars with a rubber mallet to make sure they weren't tampered with. That mallet is now referred to as the Huffington Mallet.

No one ever knows what the universe intends for them and it's a good thing that this escape wasn't successful. I ended up in the hole, solitary confinement. There was a cement slab for a bed and no windows, no view, and no other inmates to talk to. One night the guards were making their rounds and I complained to them about having horrible stomach cramps. Of course, they ignored me and left me on my own. On a later round they found me curled up on the floor, writhing in pain. My stomach was so cramped that I couldn't stretch out my legs. I didn't bother calling out for help. I knew they didn't care so I stayed silent, concentrated on breathing and controlling the pain. The sole person who can authorize a hospital visit is the assigned nurse, who was home asleep. They woke her with a phone call around 4 a.m. Lucky enough for me my temperature was miscommunicated as being 104 instead of 100.4 degrees. She told them to take me to the hospital. There, they discovered my appendix ruptured and rushed me into surgery. Had my attempted escape been successful, this might have killed me.

Returning to the Maryland State Penitentiary was different as well. I still went to the law library, but not every day. This time I started to accept prison life, but I wasn't very good at it in the beginning. I spent a lot of time on lockup and solitary confinement. I wasn't willing to adhere to the rules. I'm not a trouble-making kind of person to start with and most of the infractions were for minor violations like operating a football pool, refusing a guard's orders, or possessing contraband like football betting slips. There were a couple of unavoidable fights. Violence is common and the accepted reaction to confrontation. One was with another inmate who sucker punched me after breakfast one morning. We returned from eating breakfast and stood on the tier in front of our cells. That's when a mentally unstable inmate shoved me as he went past. When I told him to keep his hands to himself, he took a swing at me. It grazed me and we fought until the guards broke it up. The guards and the other inmates watching agreed that it was the other guy who swung at me. I was still placed in handcuffs and taken to lock-up. In normal circumstances they would have sorted it out and released me from lock-up. But as they packed up my property, they found a shank in my cell. It wasn't mine. I retrieved it the night before for a friend with intent to pass it off to him that morning. The fight threw a wrench in those plans and I got caught with it. At my adjustment hearing they found me not guilty for fighting, but guilty for the shank. I got six months in segregation for it.

I also got in a fight with an officer working my tier one evening. That one I'm still not sure how to explain. A local news station expected me for an interview. After I got back from a shower, an officer locked the tier down and wanted to shut my door. Once that happens it is difficult to get it reopened. With respect, I explained to the officer that I needed a few minutes to get dressed. The station expected me on the administrative floor for the interview. We were both in stress mode and did not communicate. It escalated from a minor argument to a push and shove, and then into a full-on fist fight. After I locked him in a headlock he agreed to end the fight and I let him go. We sort of squared off, both huffing and puffing, eying each other but that was it and it was over. We shook hands and never spoke of it afterward.

There came a point in 1986 when my attitude and outlook changed. A friend of mine who worked with me in the package room was always working on a lot of paperwork and projects. I talked to him about the things he was doing. It turned out he was a member of one of the self-help/service groups, the Junior Chamber of Commerce (Jaycees). The Jaycees is an international organization premised on leadership development through community service. I became interested in that organization and my friend encouraged me to join. They brought me right onto the board as the Ways and Means director. In that role I was in charge of fundraising for the chapter by selling various items to the prison general population like t-shirts, cookies, candies, and odds-n-ends they could use to decorate their cells.

My involvement in the Jaycees was a reawakening of a social conscience instilled in me as a child. Returning to the Pen after my second trial, my mother told me once that I must be there for a reason. I felt this was it, or that it would lead somewhere. My involvement in the Jaycees led to a pivotal change in my mentality and how I saw myself. I was becoming everything the system thought I couldn't be. I was not the picture they tried to paint of me in the media. I didn't have to feed into that narrative.

I knew I didn't help myself by violating rules and getting into trouble, so I reclaimed myself. Nobody gave a damn about the young men inside, 14 and 15-year-old boys with life sentences. Community service felt like a calling for me. I was going to care for my prison community and fellow inmates. I refused to allow prison or the penitentiary to define me. I was not going to be that person. In the Pen, I was Inmate #160-354 but my truth and my word still existed. I wasn't going to break either or live a life that didn't have meaning. I owed my parents and myself at least that.

I won the presidential election of the Old Town Jaycees in 1988. At that time there were about 120 guys involved in the organization. Despite being one of the few white men in the community at the time, I won the vote. I took that responsibility seriously. In my first duty as president, I wrote to the warden and request permission to submit an activity card, one that I developed, to the case management department for inclusion in the participating inmate's base files. Up until that point, there was no record or validation of an inmate's participation in positive programming unless they brought it with them to a parole hearing or classification process. It seemed important for these efforts to affect significant decisions such as security decreases or parole opportunities.

Through the Jaycees, we ran various programs and projects that benefited the outside community as well as ours. I remain convinced that through our efforts we changed a little bit of the mentality and environment of the penitentiary for the better. We recruited younger inmates to participate in positive programming and encouraged them to continue their education. Many earned their GEDs and some received college degrees. I used to say it was like walking through raindrops because I held the respect of both the prison administration as well as the inmate population. I was able to spearhead a lot of projects and programs that did not exist in a place like the penitentiary. There was no reason to expect it couldn't happen and I was too determined to take no for an answer. I felt made to fill this niche.

It was through our mutual involvement with the Jaycees that I met Lynn. She was beautiful, a bank officer, and well regarded throughout the organization. Of course, I felt she was out of my league. For some reason she seemed to like me though and we started seeing one another. Dating didn't apply under the circumstances, but we were both attracted to one another and that developed into a love affair that would last the remaining twenty-five years of my incarceration. A lot of guys inside tried to maintain marriages or relationships, but they didn't last. I believe ours did because I told Lynn right from the beginning to live her life. I never questioned that or tried to control her life outside. The last thing I wanted was to impose my sentence on anyone else. I was content to appreciate and value our phone calls, occasional visits, and correspondence. Knowing that she was in my life made me optimistic about the future. It kept me motivated in my fight for freedom.

In 1988 my chapter of the Jaycees teamed up with several outside organizations: the Baltimore City Jaycees, Baltimore Gas & Electric, Maryland Chapter of International Television Video

Association, and WMAR-TV to produce a video project. Scared straight types of programs operated in the prison system; however, our goal was unique. We strove to create a video product, utilizing our younger inmates, to send a message to the kids on the street, those that weren't going to come in for a scared straight program. We wanted to highlight young inmate stories and get the message to their peers on the street about peer pressure, drug use, and the consequences of that behavior. When the commissioner of corrections denied our project stating he didn't want to glorify inmates, I launched a successful letter-writing campaign and got the project reinstated. We were allowed to produce It's a Matter of Choice. By its completion, there was a new commissioner of corrections. After viewing the finished product, he liked it so much that he cosponsored a special premier night in our auditorium. Over 300 outside dignitaries attended. One of those attendees represented V103, a local R&B station, which also owned a music video program called VTV. The opening rap video, written and produced by our members, aired on their channel as a regular music video as part of VTV programming.

That wasn't to be my last foray into television. When Oprah was starting out, she co-hosted a local talk show with Richard Scher in Baltimore called People Are Talking. The channel their show aired on placed a promo ad asking for show ideas. I wrote in and suggested they do a program about life in prison and on death row. That ended up being a two day program that included life as a correctional officer.

There were other big affairs with even bigger names visiting the Pen. Sugar Ray Leonard was a bit of a regular to our boxing gym. Incarcerated with us was one of his childhood friends. I got the opportunity to meet Muhammad Ali when he made a prison visit. The show Entertainment Tonight featured the Pen and its inmates as well. Prison Fellowship arranged a concert that included Stevie Wonder and Marilyn McCoo. It was a secret from the inmate population with limits on who could attend. I knew ahead of time, but when I arrived at the auditorium it was already filled with people that Prison Fellowship bussed in. We were a little hard-pressed to find seats for ourselves. Never quite figured out exactly who that concert was for. Prison Fellowship outside volunteers were well represented and the organization received a lot of national press coverage for the event.

Around this same time, there was another convict at the Pen with a notorious reputation throughout the system, Dennis Wise. Accused of being a hitman for a large New York drug ring, Dennis established himself as a respected and influential individual within the prison hierarchy. He decided to make a more positive change and was now taking a similar path as me. Dennis was the president of the local NAACP chapter inside the prison. A lot of people in the administration thought that this was some kind of scam. However, I remembered the times I sat down and talked to him. He was for real and proved it. We discussed changes we could make together. For example, when schools were first putting kids back into uniforms because of the violence over certain clothing or shoes, we were the first to step up. In one instance, a stray bullet killed a little girl. The Jaycees joined Dennis and his NAACP group's efforts to adopt her elementary school and subsidize the cost of their uniforms. Hardened convicts, on the Penitentiary yard, donated $1 or $2 of their $30 monthly pay.

My most memorable and longest-lasting projects include creating the Family Day program and helping to bring Alternatives to Violence Project (AVP) to the Maryland Prison System. Both of which I did in 1988 and both of which still exist in every prison in the State. The same year, our volunteer activities coordinator, Cynthia Distance, called me in for a meeting. She wanted to do a special program over the Christmas holiday for the inmates and their children. She felt confident in my writing skills based on the many proposals and projects that I submitted over the years. The task given to me involved coming up with a plan that the administration would approve. Of course, I liked the challenge. I was certain that anything was possible and I went for it with a passion. We were able to secure the necessary approvals and that first year we provided a very unique Christmas for a lot of kids and men who missed out on that experience for years, and for some, decades.

We kept it small the first year, providing a Santa and plenty of toys for the kids through Prison Fellowship Ministries. The primary focus was a full contact, three hour visit for the men with their children and families in an open auditorium area with minimal supervision. For the first time, no one needed to explain to a child why they couldn't cross the visiting room barrier for a hug from their father. The joy of watching their children open presents and play with them was something to behold. For someone who has never lost those privileges it's impossible to convey the meaningfulness of this simple program to the men and their families. Children were too often overlooked in the tragedy and after-effects of incarceration, but this program changed lives. Talking to the men after was emotional and impactful as they related what that time meant for them. The next year I spent almost the entire year engaged in a letter writing campaign to solicit corporate donations. That second year we amassed a budget of $10,000 to provide toys and gifts, free pictures, buttons, face painting, popcorn, hot dogs, and other fun things. By the third year, I helped three other prisons get Family Day programs going. We also added a Father's Day program to the calendar.

Later, the administration took over the program and it brought both good and bad changes. The good part was that they made it a Division of Correction Directive (DCD), mandating that every prison hold at least one Family Day program per year. The bad was that administrators used it as a behavior modification tool. First, the guests were to be immediate family, no one else. Second, inmates now required a year, infraction-free, in order to participate. If they were a gang member they couldn't participate at all. I argued hard against the immediate family rule. Here I was, the program creator, and although I was lucky enough to have a lady in my life, a girlfriend was not considered immediate family. Under that rule, I could not participate. The administration refrained from rescinding that rule, but they blinked and I participated in these programs for the next 25 years. I worked with my guys at the button-making station and it was amazing to watch "our" little kids grow up through the years into young adults. Each year they came by the station to say "Merry Christmas" to Mr. John & Mr. Johnny.

The second program was the Alternatives to Violence Project (AVP). This was a conflict resolution program started with the help of the Quakers in Greenhaven State Prison, New York, in the late seventies. The program consisted of a three day weekend and was a combination of inmates and outside participants. A team of three to five facilitators ran the workshops and both inmates and outside participants would attend as equals. There are three segments to the program starting with a three day basic weekend. If one liked that, then they could sign up to attend a three-day advanced weekend. For those with the desire, they could continue on to take the three day Trainer For Trainers workshop and become facilitators themselves. I was one of the first trained inmate facilitators and went on to conduct more workshops than I can count. This program is one of the most impactful and worthwhile things I was ever a part of and I still carry with me its philosophies and lessons.

I found out the extent of that impact on me several years down the road. A young Black guy came into the Pen and seemed to be trying to make a name for himself by fighting white inmates. Somehow, he thought he could make a name for himself off me and I got on his radar. He came at me one night during recreation time in the housing unit, but the moment wasn't right for a full-on confrontation. Instead, he called me out to meet him in the school building the next morning. Prison rules are different from the outside, and a public challenge was unavoidable. Now neither of us could walk away from it. To show any type of weakness or backing down from a physical challenge, created additional problems. Once a weakness revealed itself, inmates exploited it. In prison, everyone watches everything and vulnerabilities require defending. I established myself right from the moment I came into the prison and carried a lot of respect. However, I had to face a physical confrontation at one point. In the Pen, if there's beef then it's time to strap up and go at it. No matter how non-violent an inmate does their time, they pretty much need a shank either stashed away or accessible. That night I got mine out and prepared myself mentally to survive. I didn't want to do this but I didn't have a choice.

The next morning I went to the school building first, entered an empty classroom, and waited. I asked a friend to stay positioned in the silk screen shop next door to make sure no one else got involved and this stayed one-on-one. Twenty minutes later my challenger showed up and came into the classroom. He shut the door behind him and walked to the front. I was standing in the back of the classroom with my hand on my knife, which was still in my dip (waistband). He glanced at me, pulled on a pair of gloves, and waved me on. His impression that this was somehow a fist fight flustered me for a moment. Then I pulled out my knife and charged him. The fear in his eyes was unforgettable when he realized that this wasn't playtime. There was a flash of fear as he glanced toward the door that he came through, now closed. We both knew he would not reach it and even if he did, it opened inward. It's amazing how many thoughts can flash through your mind in a nanosecond. All the while I was in motion. As I swung that knife straight at his head my AVP training seemed to kick in. At the last second I turned my hand and hit him with my fist. I violated every rule of the jungle and I knew it, but I knew I couldn't take a life. At that moment, a friend of his kicked open the door and he ran out. I followed him into the hallway still unsure of what I was going to do. We squared off for a few minutes at either end of the hallway before he fled down the stairs. I went into the silk screen shop to regroup. My friends came in to say he was out looking for a weapon. He never came back but sent word that night that he wanted to squash the beef. That was a tough one for him because he faced a lot of peer pressure after he ran from a white boy with a knife. However, he learned who I was and didn't want any further issues. The two of us met the next day and I was able to tell him that it was AVP that saved his life – and mine as well. In truth, neither one of us wanted to kill or die and there were other ways to settle our differences. He signed up for an AVP workshop a couple of months after our altercation.

For me, it was a brutal awakening that no matter how far I came on my personal journey, day-to-day life was going to be tough inside. I followed its rules or I wouldn't survive. I also found that I could lead by example and show others that there was gray, not black and white, to the law of the land. I maintained my respect and standing without following blindly into the call of the darkness. Prison might be the worst place imaginable to find one's humanity, but it's possible if done in truth and righteousness. It comes down to situational awareness in a sense. Not to minimize or ignore the gravity of the situation but place it in a perspective that is decipherable to survive it and, in some cases, thrive and succeed in spite of it. Viewing my life's situations as challenges rather than setbacks was the first step. Understanding that there are things I cannot change allowed a progression into positive thoughts. What I could do with those challenges or in spite of them? One can be a cockroach and survive everything or a unicorn that surpasses circumstances. For me, I took on the attitude that prison walls did not need to define me. I did not accept the status quo and took steps that changed me and as many of my surroundings as possible. Respect is a big deal in prison but, more often than not, it's misdefined and misapplied. AVP teaches us transforming powers and provides a tool belt to de-escalate violent situations and I stand in testimony that this program works.

I won numerous terms as president of the Jaycees chapters, both in the penitentiary and at another prison in Jessup, Maryland. I was also on the Inmate Advisory Council (IAC) which served as the liaison between the inmate population and the administration. In that role, we were able to stop and avoid a major prison riot in 1989. There's a quote by Charles Dudley Warner that stood out to me and couldn't be truer.

*"It is one of the beautiful compensations of this life that no one can sincerely try to help another without helping himself."*

The years began to blend together. I tried to stay involved in positive programming, get my education, and I continued fighting my legal battle through countless appeals and court systems. I never accepted my situation, but I tried to make my life have some meaning, some purpose.

In 1988, the United States Supreme Court made a ruling in another Maryland death penalty case. In State v. Mills, the high court ruled that for years Maryland administered the death penalty sentencing process in an unconstitutional manner. This ruling resulted in the need to grant everyone on death row at the time a re-sentencing hearing. In a death penalty sentencing, it boils down to a numbers game. Do the mitigating circumstances outweigh the aggravating circumstances? The Supreme Court ruled that it was unconstitutional to place the burden of proof on the defendant to prove mitigating circumstances. The prosecutor in my case, Joseph Cassilly, knew a death penalty review is more stringent and that attorneys are keener to assist in a capital case as compared to a "regular" life sentence. He elected not to pursue the death penalty and figured that I would vanish in the annals of time and lose my support system. After ten years I came off of death row to serve two consecutive life sentences.

# CHAPTER 7

Once I straightened my path, I found the opportunity to earn my college degree. When I first went into the penitentiary, Coppin State University offered four-year degrees. I started classes, majoring in math with a minor in computer science; however, before I finished my first semester, I took time off and devoted my time to my case. I did not have the capacity to focus on college as well. After about ten years, I made the decision to go back. The offerings changed but our college program included several HBCUs, two offered Associate of Arts degrees with Coppin State University offering Bachelor of Science degrees. I enrolled at CSU in 1992 as a degree seeking candidate for a Bachelor's degree in management science and gained approval to seek another BS degree in applied psychology.

Three weeks into the first semester our World History professor sprung a pop quiz on us. At thirty-two years of age with a thirteen year gap since last attending school, I carried a high degree of test anxiety. When I aced that pop quiz, I realized that the educational experience was not the same as when I was in high school and community college. I was absorbing information like a sponge. I wanted to learn. I knew that I had more to prove than any regular student. I needed more than a piece of paper saying I obtained a degree. I needed knowledge and education. Wherever life took me I would operate at a disadvantage. The equalizer was to have a true education. From that moment on I never looked back or missed a class and I was on time with every one of my assignments. It was not enough to pass an exam. I sought 100s or high 90s.

I jumped from taking seventeen credits that the first semester to maxing out at twenty-one credits each semester. I finished every semester with straight As. It turns out, it was lucky for me that I chose to do that much work.

In 1994, Congress passed a crime bill, which included the removal of Pell Grant eligibility from prison inmates. The purpose of Pell Grant programs was to aid students with financial need without requiring repayment. Incarcerated individuals fit the specific criteria and this grant allowed funding for the Institutional College Programs. The enactment of this law ended the program within a year. Inmate participation in prison based college education dropped by almost half within a year.

Spring of 1995 was to be my last semester enrolled in Coppin State University. Because I took the maximum credits every semester, I graduated as a junior. After I completed six semesters I was able to fulfill my degree requirements for a Bachelor of Science in management science, with a concentration in economics and finance. This did not come easy. For my last semester, I took a full course load of 21 credits and challenged two additional required courses by examination. That meant I studied and prepared myself for both of those courses without any instruction. I sat for one final exam that covered the entire course. Though I did not achieve a second bachelor's degree, I earned a minor in applied psychology. I was on the Dean's List every semester and named class valedictorian. I earned the highest GPA for the entire class of 1995 at Coppin State and was named valedictorian for the inside portion of the program. Participation in the official campus graduation ceremonies was not allowed.

This was one of my proudest moments. I felt like I achieved something important and I wanted to make my parents proud. Especially my father. The graduation ceremony was a family affair for me. I was allowed ten guests. My parents, sister Pam and her husband Brian, my niece and nephew, my girlfriend, two of my Jaycees' friends, and my attorney attended. For weeks I worked on the decorations for the auditorium by myself. I also prepared programs and arranged the menu.

I delivered the valedictorian speech where I extolled the benefit of having educational opportunities while incarcerated. I attempted to convey the effort and dedication that it took for my fellow graduates to achieve these diplomas and their value to us. Prison presents many obstacles to those seeking to find rehabilitation through educational programs and it is a noteworthy achievement to fulfill these goals. Staying out of and away from trouble is necessary and difficult while seeking a four-year degree in prison. The political push to restrict the Pell Grants was campaign rhetoric fed to a misinformed public. It is easy to stroke someone's ire by stating the obvious of what it costs for parents to send their kids to college versus a convicted offender receiving a "free" education. Did removing the inmates' access to the Pell Grant somehow lower the costs of tuition for the regular tax-paying citizen? Quite the contrary. In fact, education is key to reducing recidivism. If inmates maintained access to higher education, the estimate of resulting reductions in criminal recidivism would have saved states over $365 million per year in incarceration costs.

I lived this for 32 years of my life. My achievements listed above are not for self-aggrandizement. It is an illustration of the women and men who have pursued higher education while incarcerated. Many of them have achieved higher degrees such as master's degrees. They represented a minority of the prison population who sought educational opportunities, but they have proven the most successful in reintegrating into society when given that opportunity. My return and reintegration provided me with many opportunities and blessings, none of which would have been possible without my educational foundation and the opportunities that were available to me while incarcerated.

I have a successful career and serve on several non-profit boards as well as the governor's task force and several business-lead work groups. For five years I was the director of the largest community-based reentry program and worked to help men and women reintegrate and receive job training and workforce development.

In my experience there is overwhelming anecdotal evidence to support the role education played in readiness, adaptability, and successful reintegration for those individuals given the opportunity to receive an education while incarcerated.

Today, I serve as the director of business development for a financial services company, Kinetic Capital, LLC. I work in the field of my degree, but it wasn't that piece of paper that got me there. It was the education that piece of paper represents. It was the hunger and thirst for knowledge and betterment of self that I shared with others who sought their path from behind the walls. Education was the key to unlocking the prison gates.

*"With education comes empowerment; with empowerment, confidence. And when you're confident, you can succeed."* – John Huffington

I tried focusing on the positivity of the activities and the work I immersed myself in while incarcerated, but nothing erased the nightmare of prison. Prison was a world where violence was currency and life had no value. Inmates woke up in the morning and girded themselves with their masks. Convicts were the best in the world at reading people and they smelled weakness without difficulty. Each weakened individual meant opportunities for exploitation. The population guarded their words, their eye contact, and body language. When I learned of the passing of my mother in 2009 it was one of the hardest moments of my life. I sought out the one place I could be alone, the bathroom of the office where I worked, and I punched the air in silent grief. I wanted to cry, I wanted to scream out to the world, but I couldn't. I composed myself before walking out. The stony look in my eyes and the rocks in my jaw showed I was unapproachable. The prison system stopped compassionate leaves more than a decade earlier which meant I wasn't going to attend her funeral or visit her grave site. My five minutes in that bathroom beating the shit out of the air was all I had. My temporary respite was the final lock-in for the night. When the cell door slammed shut and the lock hit, there were around eight hours before it started over. There wasn't much of a reprieve while in a six by nine foot cell with another man. Cells contained a bunk bed and a combination toilet/sink. Most folks' bathrooms are bigger than that. As long as an inmate and their cell buddy were cool, they could relax to a small degree. It was a time to get lost in memories and thoughts. Memories are what sustained me. Thoughts I was more careful with. While I fought for my freedom, at no time would I allow myself to daydream about a future. I watched too many guys lose focus on reality. They either got too comfortable and accepted the prison lifestyle or went off the deep end because they couldn't cope. Inmates called the latter zap-outs. They'd do the Thorazine shuffle out in the yard having lost their sanity.

There's a famous quote by Nietzsche, "That which does not kill us makes us stronger." While I agree with that, there's a lesser known quote by him that stuck with me more, "He who has a why to live can bear almost any how.

# CHAPTER 8

Over thirty-two years I must have seen it all. Murders, stabbings, a standoff between two inmates on the tier, both of
them pointing guns at each other, men burned alive, and every
senseless act of violence and depravity imaginable. I lived in two
different institutions where a correctional officer died at the
hands of an inmate. I've been through two prison riots and a
shoot-out on the wall between inmates trying to escape and the
guards trying to prevent it. In 1989 several inmates smuggled
in guns and took over an entire building for days, an incident
now known as Desert Storm as it ended with every inmate
brought out of the building butt naked and then housed in the
yard in National Guard tents. The guns were never found. The
Penitentiary was too old. There were too many hiding places and
blind spots which contributed to the life-threatening environment. One walkway through the yard picked up the nicknamed
Blood Alley for the amount of violence that occurred on it.
Another walkway earned the nickname the Sawdust Trail for

close to the same reason and because of the sawdust used to soak up the blood.

I spent my first sixteen years of incarceration in the Maryland State Penitentiary. When I first went in there were a lot of neighborhood cliques; East vs. West Baltimore, Baltimore vs. DC. Today, most major gangs have a presence. BGF, 5%'ers, Murder Inc., Bloods, Crips, MS13, Latin Kings, Pagans, Phantoms. Dead Man, Inc. (DMI), touted as one of the largest prison gangs in the country, began in Maryland with a couple of friends of mine. I chose to stay unaffiliated but made friends at the highest leadership levels of each of these organizations.

During the first stint in the Pen before my retrial, I clerked for the 8-4 shift major. My boss was also the executioner for the state. If my sentence was ever carried out, it would be by him. Major Sven Hanson was his name and he was a pretty fair and reasonable man. We got along fine. He was in the movie, And Justice For All, starring Al Pacino. There were several scenes filmed in the penitentiary. A hostage scene in the movie came to an end when a guard posted on the tower shoots the inmate. After killing the inmate, the guard takes off his helmet. That was Major Hanson in his acting debut.

When I came back to the penitentiary from my second trial I was the package clerk in the property room. From that job, I went on to become the clerk for the VAC (Volunteer Activities Coordinator) where a phone with an outside line sat right on my desk. That, I put to full advantage in strengthening and expanding our volunteer resources. I also worked in the silk screen shop. The organization I was president of, the Old Town Jaycees, owned and operated it. We were able to create unique designs, secure contracts, and function as a business. Of course, our finances went through the institution but we had free reign other than that. When the penitentiary closed as a maximum-security institution in 1995 we shipped out to other institutions. I went to Cumberland at that time. Before I left, I contacted FACETS Boys Home in Harford County and offered to donate the Silk Screen Shop to them as a job training opportunity for the boys as well as a fundraiser for the organization. They sent a couple of their personnel to spend a few days with us learning how to do it. Then a friend of mine, who ran a moving company, came down, got everything, and delivered it to them.

From the Pen, it was out to nowhere land in the mountains of Cumberland County. There I learned what the term *eyeballin'* meant. The correctional officers, or hillbillies to the inmates, didn't like for us to make eye contact with them and prisoners would get called out, "Why are you eyeballin' me, boy?" The hillbillies had another peculiar pet peeve: the inmates better not walk on their grass. They kept their prison complex as well-groomed as that type of place can be. They would get incensed if inmates strayed off the concrete pathway and stepped on their grass. The guards accosted anyone who did it and issued them a notice of infraction. They were fine if we wanted to kill each other but don't dare walk on the grass. I could not exist in the good ol' boy world of Cumberland. It was too racist and non-progressive for me. I started a couple of programs there but everything was an uphill battle. Even if the administration approved a program or activity, the guard force discouraged it by delaying or losing approvals or in any other way imaginable.

Lucky for me, I spent very little time there before my transfer to the Cutt in Jessup. Prison staff thought I was crazy for wanting to go to the Cutt because it boasted a terrible reputation. The original source of its nickname came from its geographical location, cut through a mountainous region for what was a railroad track. Over time, it grew into its nickname's current meaning as it became well-known for its level of violence and number of stabbings. The shock trauma helicopter did a lot of flying there. Built as part tiers (cells) and part dormitories, those dorms were infamous for continuous violence. The back dorms of the Cutt, which housed over 100 inmates each, were H, I, and J Dorm. Or as we knew them, Hell Dorm, Insane Dorm, and Jungle Dorm. The Cutt was where I went to work for MCE (Maryland Correctional Enterprises). MCE asked me to come to work for them when I was in the penitentiary but at the time I liked my jobs and freedom of movement compared to that world.

When I first went to the Cutt, I was a clerk in the education department but a friend recruited me to take his spot as the clerk for the tag plant. The tag plant is a $5.4 million a year operation and yes, like in the movies, they make all the license plates for the state. It was a great job for me. Compared to the $30 per month that prison jobs paid, MCE paid a base rate plus incentive pay. I made about $150 per month. Convicts call that lawyer money because it lets you save money for a lawyer.

I worked in the tag plant for 10 years and it allowed me the opportunity to hone my business skills. Along with production reports, I managed the payroll, inventory, and office. I could hone my artistic skills there as well. In the Pen and the Cutt, I painted huge scenic backdrops for different functions and happenings in the prison. No convicts wanted to take pictures in front of steel bars or concrete walls. The artwork was at least fifteen by twelve feet, made up of different scenes: cityscape, ocean, winter wonderland, and so on. My biggest work was for my college graduation. Coppin State's mascot is an eagle so I painted the mascot on a twenty-seven foot by fourteen-foot backdrop that covered the movie screen in our auditorium where the graduations occur. I found a lot of peace in painting. I did a couple of oils, a pastel, and several in pen and ink.

In our silk screen shop in the penitentiary, I learned how to prepare artwork by hand for production and do color separation for silk screening. We would take rub-off Chartpak lettering to do any wording and then with hand-cut film, we would use Exacto knives to cut out each letter in the film. In the tag plant, I gained access to computer-aided sign software that I adapted to use in a short time. I developed such efficiency that my boss held my finished artwork before sending it to the customer because he didn't want clients to get used to such a fast turnaround time. I was so good at it, that the neighboring sign plant would bring me their artwork to do as well.

At this point, I thought I was doing all the right things. I was still president of the Jaycees chapter in the Cutt, head clerk of the biggest MCE plant in the prison system, served on the IAC, and helped to run both AVP and the Family Day programs. I maintained a stellar 13-year track record without a single rule infraction. But here, I found out that no good deed goes unpunished, and none of it would matter.

In 1999 we awoke one morning to an invasion. I lived in D Dormitory and our windows faced the front parking lot. We got word a shakedown was coming and as we watched from the windows, we saw bus upon bus of correctional officers unloading. They were in full riot gear: helmets, vests, knee pads, batons, and some with shotguns. Busload after busload unloaded. They formed up and marched into the institution like army troops in formation. We learned later that in this search and seizure, called Operation '99, the Department of Corrections deployed over nine hundred correctional officers. State troopers assisted by cordoning off the perimeter of the institution. They were there for one purpose. Seize Dennis Wise from the Penitentiary. He was the President of the NAACP chapter back in the 80s. The correction officials claim that he was the "Godfather" and ran the Cutt (MD House of Correction) and they feared a riot if they tried to remove him without this overwhelming amount of police presence. They grabbed Dennis and an additional forty-nine inmates they claimed were part of his group or exerted influence inside. A phalanx of officers escorted me to the commissary area where they stripped us, put us into orange jumpsuits and three-pieces (handcuffs, belly chain, and leg irons), then placed us onto buses headed to SuperMax in Baltimore.

Today, over two-thirds of states now have SuperMax - maximum security prisons. The most famous is Red Onion in Virginia followed by Pelican Bay in California. In the early 80s, correctional staff from various states visited those prisons and brought the SuperMax concepts back to their home states. In theory, they're designed to hold the putative most violent and disruptive inmates in single-cell confinement for 23 hours per day, often for an indefinite period of time. However, they've been a lightning rod for controversy, in particular the unconstitutionality of this type of confinement and its severe psychological effects on those confined within. SuperMax prisons across the country housed plenty of infamous prisoners, including Ted Kaczynski (Unibomber), Joaquin "El Chapo" Guzman, Terry Nichols (Oklahoma City Bombing), Robert Hanssen (FBI double agent/spy), Ramzi Yousef and Mohammed Salameh (World Trade Center bombers), Richard Reid (Shoe Bomber) and John Gotti (Mafia).

The inmate population was well aware of SuperMax. Everyone knew a few guys who ended up with stints there, but I was at a loss to understand why I was there. Even more confusing was that they told us that we were under investigation as a threat to the Cutt.

There is no set time frame for a stint in SuperMax. Dennis Wise and two other guys transferred to other states. Dennis would do the rest of his time in the Arizona state prison system. Among the rest of us, they assigned forty-four guys status reviews in six months. Two other guys and I picked up one full year before our review. Efforts by my family, who contacted our senator and the governor's office, produced no answers on why I was there. The acting commissioner's response to my mother was, "He knows why he's there." I ended up doing a year and a half in SuperMax without ever knowing why.

At the end of the first week, I was there, I experienced the darkest moment of my incarceration. I couldn't wrap my head around what led to me being in SuperMax or why. I was angry and frustrated. I started questioning the good and positive things that I accomplished over the past thirteen years. If it meant nothing, then why did I do it and what would be the point in continuing? I hit my personal wall. I stared into the abyss and it stared back at me. Late one evening, after midnight, I reached my breaking point. I didn't have it in me to keep going or to keep fighting my case or a system that didn't care at all. I started to consider ending my life and wondered if I possessed the courage to do it.

I started having a conversation in my head with my mom, apologizing for the mountain of grief I caused her in my life and tried to explain why I didn't have it in me to keep going. I was asking for her forgiveness when my cell door clanged open. On the other side stood two guards and a sergeant yelling Shakedown! They came to search my cell, but I realized I knew the sergeant from the Pen. I often exchanged pleasantries with him while waiting in line at the commissary. Here he was now, this smiley motherfucker looking back at me with no clue of the thoughts in my head. He heard I was there and came by to pay his respects. He used the absurdity of a shakedown as a reason to come to the cell and it shook me back into reality. We chatted for a few minutes and he left.

I accepted that the universe talks to us in subtle ways, and this encounter seemed to be a loud and clear message. It came at the lowest, most depressing moment in my life. I don't know that I would have done anything, but very dark thoughts crept into my mind. At that moment, his visit re-energized me. It made me more determined to live and prove my innocence. I wasn't done until I achieved that. From that moment forward I refused to allow myself near the abyss. I wouldn't make the connection until fourteen years later but the moment of my darkest hour, when I came closest to giving up, should have been a moment of revelation about the evidence in my case being in doubt.

I arrived at SuperMax in 1999 – the same year the FBI told the prosecuting attorney in my case that there were issues with the evidence in my trial.

# CHAPTER 9

Life in SuperMax is the bare minimum. All personal property like my TV, radio, typewriter, and clothing went home and were not allowed back. The few items allowed inside were my legal paperwork and photos. It's total isolation. Perpetual fluorescent lighting replaced fresh air and sunlight.

There's not much to keep the mind active. The options are either go nuts or impose self-discipline. I kept to a regular calisthenics routine and tried to keep my mind active doing things like crossword puzzles. It was the sheer force of will and determination to maintain my sanity. Confined to their cells, inmates are alone for at least 23 hours a day. Often, inmates spent the full twenty-four-hour day inside their cells, as officers didn't get around to providing recreation or a shower. When I did get rec time, it occurred in dog cages like the ones seen in prison movies. They are enclosures set up inside of a yard surrounded by walls so high that it was impossible to see the outside or feel the sun because of the roof on the cage. It wasn't much bigger than my cell and there was nothing to do but pace.

The food was inedible and it was difficult to supplement meals with commissary items. Because choices were limited, I accumulated little to nothing. The main commissary purchase was peanut butter and jelly. I ate peanut butter and jelly sandwiches for lunch and dinner for a year and a half. The staff used food as a behavioral modification tool. If an inmate violated any of the institutional rules, the punishment was being placed on the loaf. Its official name is Nutraloaf. It is like meatloaf in texture but looks and smells like dog food. It has a wide variety of ingredients like vegetables, fruit, meat, and bread or other grains. It's considered a complete meal. Once on the loaf, it's the only food provided for meals three times a day. When I left SuperMax after eighteen months, I suffered from severe irritable bowel syndrome.

During my time there, my classification status was ER (escape risk) because of my attempted escape in 1984. That meant that I received a shake-down every shift on a daily basis and that they moved me to a different cell every three to four days. I started to lose my hair. Every day, I cleaned up large clumps of my hair from the cell floor. That was embarrassing and I made sure to clean every bit up before they moved me to the next cell.

SuperMax experienced more than its share of corruption. The Feds tried to investigate it but inside authorities denied entrance over and over. When they finally gained entrance, they discovered a number of constitutional violations. These included cruel and unusual punishment, such as in the notorious "Pink Room" where correctional staff beat inmates. Admins denied medical care and confined inmates to inhumane lengths of isolation. There were incidents of inmate-on-inmate violence despite claims this was a prison that eliminated physical contact between prisoners. In October of 2020, the United States Attorney's office indicted nine defendants on federal charges in an alleged racketeering scheme to smuggle in contraband, including narcotics, tobacco, and cell phones. That indictment included three correctional officers.

Baltimore prisons have a long history of corruption and complicity amongst their correctional staff. Right after my transfer out of SuperMax, one inmate killed another in front of a guard shack. Despite an unrestricted view of the entire area, not a guard intervened or saw anything. In April of 2012, the state entered into a contract with the Feds. Converted to hold federal, pre-trial detainees, SuperMax rebranded under its new name, Chesapeake Detention Facility. Oddly enough, I handled the contract to convert their signage over to the new name in my role as clerk for the sign plant.

I spent a year and a half there before getting released to Jessup Correctional Institution (JCI), a maximum security facility. I wasn't allowed to return to the Cutt. When I got to JCI, I was placed in administrative segregation and told I was a threat to the security of the institution. I told the review board that I was never in their institution, how could I be a threat? If they felt that way and were going to keep me on lockdown then they might as well put me back on the bus to SuperMax. Somehow that argument made sense to them and they approved me for release into the general population.

I spent almost a year in JCI when the upper-level administration of the division of corrections changed and there was a new commissioner. His director of operations, James Peguese, was the former security chief at the Cutt when I got sent to SuperMax. Director Peguese happened to be visiting JCI one day and I was able to ask him about what happened. He informed me that I got caught up in politics within the department. The individual behind Operation '99 was vying for the title of Commissioner. He was no longer a part of the division of corrections and the new commissioner revoked my restriction from returning to the Cutt.

The system returned me to the Cutt the day after New Year's in 2004 and regained my position in the Maryland Correctional Enterprises' tag plant. During the time I was away, the division of corrections eliminated many of the inmate organizations with the exception of Alcoholics Anonymous, Narcotics Anonymous, the Veterans, and AVP. Without the Jaycees, I went back to AVP and ran the Family Day programs and found the institution changed for the worse. Violence levels increased and without the positive organizations to recruit and participate in, the gangs rose more prominent and they acted bolder in their activities. This culminated in the stabbing murder of a correctional officer in 2006 that shut down the Cutt. The Governor declared that it would remain closed forever and, in keeping his word, he demolished it. All the inmates were shipped out to other prisons.

After the officer's death, the prison administration brought the MCE plants back on line. Restaffing at the tag plant happened first with a skeleton crew of essential inmate workers. The tag plant needed to come back on line for production as it is the sole source of license plates for the state. A mistake allowed me to come back to work. My presence on the Inmate Advisory Council (IAC) made elements of the administration nervous. They wanted me shipped out to the far corners of the state. The administration asked the plant manager to provide a list of 15 crucial inmate workers needed in order to operate the plant. He requested me but the prison administration denied it. I was not allowed to be included. But in the end, I slipped through. A lieutenant in charge of the essential workers made a mistake. He took the alphabetically-arranged list of inmate workers (called a count-out) for the tag plant. Since my last name starts with an H, I was high enough up on the count-out from which the lieutenant grabbed the first 15 names.

The administration wanted to blame someone for the officer's death. In reality, fellow officers set him up by sending him up on the tier by himself when he wasn't supposed to be working inside the prison in inmate-accessible areas. The IAC was an easy target for the officers looking for a scapegoat to deflect attention. It felt like there was an intent to punish or blame me for being in a leadership role. But fate intervened through a clerical mistake. I made the list of inmate workers for the plant and we transferred next door, back to JCI. This whole incident gave me pause and I felt it was time to make a change. It was apparent that there were elements in the administration that opposed me. I was certain that although this attempt was unsuccessful, they would find a way to move me out of leadership.

Another of the MCE plants, the sign plant, decided to transfer its whole operation to a separate institution in Jessup called Patuxent Institution. Patuxent wasn't a part of the normal division of corrections prisons. It was co-managed by a warden and a director and staffed with doctors and therapists. To get accepted there, an inmate needed a court referral or self-applied. In either instance, there was a six-month evaluation period prior to acceptance. The advantage of admittance into their program was that inmates were no longer part of the Maryland parole system. Patuxent's own community board of review decided the time of their release, which in most instances was a lot less time than the regular system.

The rationale for the sign plant's move to Patuxent was the plant's outside contracts. The constant lockdowns of the regular prison affected the plant's ability to meet strict deadlines and contractual obligations with customers like M&T Stadium, Camden Park, MD Lottery, BWI, and other state agencies. Contracts with those entities required deliverables with can't miss deadlines. The deal was that the sign plant could bring twelve inmate workers to Patuxent. These twelve, called leadmen in MCE, ran the work crews assigned to the various segments of production. Leadmen fulfilled the role of production supervisors and quality control for their specific areas and were responsible for the work output of the inmates they supervised. Patuxent inmates worked in two shifts, one morning and one afternoon shift. The leadmen were responsible for training these inmates and kept production schedules on time with a four hour workforce. The Leadmen were the best at their job and required excellent institutional adjustment histories.

There were about thirty-five inmates working in the plant. The twenty-three who were not chosen to go to Patuxent went to other institutions or, if they were lucky, got placed in one of the other MCE plants. After expressing my interest to go, I was fortunate enough to be one of the twelve selected and transferred to Patuxent. While there, I took a writing class and wrote this essay:

My Greatest Fear

My greatest fear is to have not lived a life that had meaning and purpose. There is no greater gift than life and with that comes the freedom of choice to either squander or honor that gift.

There is a quote attributed to Plato which is, "the unexamined life is not worth living." Maybe because of my circumstances I've always taken that quote more to heart and incorporated it into my own personal philosophy. At the age of eighteen I was sentenced to death for a crime I did not commit. My initial reactions were to be expected – disbelief, shock and most definitely anger. For the next seven years or so I rebelled against everything and probably became the very stereotype I was rebelling against.

Fortunately for me, others saw something in me that I no longer thought existed and persuaded me to join the Jaycees – a leadership development organization immersed in community service. There I rediscovered the ability to engage in positive activities and programs. There I found my voice again and rediscovered my social conscience. In the process of this introspection and growth I had my epiphany that I needed to honor and not squander my gift of life. That regardless of my circumstances, there is a difference between living life and doing life.

For the past twenty-one years I've redirected my energy toward making a difference in my life, my immediate surroundings and the community at large and this is a journey that I continue on today. I was able to earn my college degree and participate in further educational opportunities. I've also been fortunate to participate in a large variety of positive programs and projects and even create several of my own. Some of those, like raising the necessary funds for a 7-year old to get life saving surgery and creating the Family Day Program, will long outlast me. And, in that – maybe in my own small way, I've hopefully left my footprint.

It's said that everything happens for a reason and a wise man will adapt to his circumstances the way water adapts to a glass. While I will never accept my current circumstances, there is a way to constructively rebel while still maintaining my humanity and furthering my personal journey. In fact, it becomes more of a moral victory to look at all I have achieved in spite of my circumstances and know that the penitentiary is walls and bars – it does not define or confine me.

For us all, it comes down to two dates on a tombstone – this man was born and this man died and few ask why or note the in-between. No matter what I do, or how hard I try to accomplish these goals, my greatest fear remains that I will fall short.

The irony of that essay was that it got me kicked out of the writing class. Patuxent is a therapeutic prison in which inmates are in a therapy program. The doctor who ran the writing class told me it was one of the best essays she ever read, but it seemed to bring up deep emotions that might require therapy. Since I wasn't in the therapy program it was best not to open those doors. Good thing I have thick skin or it might have scarred me and kept me from writing this book.

Patuxent wasn't the country club we expected. The institution was reluctant to honor the promised privileges. Instead, the administration isolated and ostracized us. In the first week alone we accumulated over 50 hours of overtime. I helped design the physical layout of the plant. While we were building walls, running electricity, etc. We kept production going. All in all, it still turned out to be the best move I ever made. I took to all aspects of the business of sign making, reading every trade magazine I could get my hands on and studying substrates and materials.

My boss left me to my own devices. Soon, I was the sole point of contact for customers. I developed the job, priced the job, ordered the materials, and shepherded the project through the specific phases of production. When customers or vendors came to visit the plant, it was my desk they sat at and me whom they met. My boss rarely if ever sat in.

Our incentive pay base was 4% of sales. I encouraged the other leadmen as we started setting record sales months. My boss and his bosses added new product lines at my recommendation. An oversized 3-ring binder filled up with the articles I read about vehicle wraps in the trade magazines we received at the plant. When an opportunity came to wrap the car of the state coordinator of the D.A.R.E. Program, I was able to convince the higher-ups to let us do it. After completing the car with my friend Chuck Grierson, who I handpicked to help with the job, I trained a larger crew to do vehicle wraps. We went on to wrap buses and lots of other vehicles. The sign plant was making an average of $600k a year and along with the help of my other leadmen, I was able to take us to $1.4 million a year. Aside from the business experience and financial boost, the biggest takeaway for me from that experience was the network I was able to develop.

MCE sales are restricted to other state agencies or non-profits. This included both our professional football & baseball stadiums, the Park Services, BWI Airport, and the MD Lottery. This network created relationships and friendships that have remained steadfast to today.

# CHAPTER 10

My case went through decades of appeals and legal proceedings. The system's design ensnares and enslaves people, it does not release them. One of my appeals in particular stuck out as an example of the fallacy of the system. In the late 80's I got a new attorney, David O. Stewart, who was with a DC law firm. David came to be my attorney through a court appointment because he desired to work on a death penalty case. Lucky for me, that case was mine. After researching the history and proceedings of my case, David realized that there were serious issues with my prosecution and conviction. This, and through our evolving relationship, would lead him to the belief that I was innocent and was wrongfully convicted. David was a top-notch attorney, one of the very best, and he brought his skills to bear in attacking my convictions and situation with unrelenting vigor and commitment. So much so that within a few years, when Ropes & Gray offered him a partnership, he made my case a part of his package deal. He would join Ropes & Gray if they accepted his continued representation of me pro bono - meaning for free. Ropes & Gray accepted that condition and has honored that commitment for now well over 35 years.

David spent quite a bit of time researching my case and filed what's called a Post Conviction in 1987-88. This is an appeal filed in circuit court rather than the normal court of appeals. We held a hearing in the Frederick County Circuit Court where we presented our case and numerous witnesses. One of those witnesses, Dr. Vincent Guinn, flew in from California to testify. He invented the Composite Bullet Lead Composition test and he taught the FBI how to use it. Dr. Guinn testified that the FBI conducted the incorrect tests; therefore, the results that the prosecution's star FBI witness testified to were invalid. After several days in court, listening to witnesses and testimony, the hearing concluded and the judge stated he would be issuing his opinion in due time. It took over three and a half years before he would issue his ruling, and when he did, it was not in my favor. Three and a half years of waiting, wondering, hoping. I remember the start of the Gulf War. The world was in turmoil, we were at war, and my case sat on the judge's desk somewhere in a dusty pile of papers. Nearly fifteen years later, the FBI announced that it would cease using this test altogether. It was determined that there were too many variables between the manufacture and distribution of bullets for accurate data to be obtained. The path to my release was long, stressful, and at times surreal. My life hung in the balance of a hair.

There is one attribute that a lot of convicts share and that's the ability to read people. It's almost a requirement, as inmates must survive in such a volatile environment. We got pretty good at knowing who is innocent after having been around each other for decades. I had a friend, Chris Conover, who was innocent himself. In the early 2000s, the National Innocence Project out of New York accepted his case. The main evidence in his case was like mine, a hair sample. When DNA testing was conducted, the results showed conclusively that it wasn't Chris' hair. The prosecutors and attorneys in Chris' case then entered into negotiations to gain his release. It was at that time he came to me to talk to me since he knew that hair evidence was critical in my case. He urged me to request DNA testing in my case and made the introductions to Nina Morrison at the National Innocence Project. Without Chris, I don't know if I would have pursued this opportunity. He and I were friends for years. I truly appreciated that friendship. Chris obtained his release in 2003 but was unable to readjust to society. He ended up taking his own life in 2015. RIP soldier.

In 2003, my legal team at Ropes & Gray, headed up by Ryan Malone, filed a petition on my behalf to secure DNA testing on the hair evidence in my case. This was the crucial piece of material evidence the state used in prosecuting me. The state led us to believe from the start that two hairs were allegedly found at the crime scene. FBI agent Michael Malone testified that he conducted the microscopic hair examination and that those hairs belonged to me to the exclusion of all others. Even though, at the time, science could not differentiate between males versus females. DNA testing didn't become available in the United

States until 1987, so during my 1981 and 1983 trials, no scientific method existed to challenge the FBI's findings. Once it did, my defense team jumped on it.

DNA testing law in Maryland required me to petition the court's permission and personally pay for the testing if the court allowed it. The tests in my case amounted to about $15,000. No small sum for someone who spent twenty-two years incarcerated. When my lawyers filed our petition, Cassilly's response, in writing, was to petition the court for permission to destroy the hair evidence. That seemed odd at the time, as DNA would simply reveal the truth. There is no way to manipulate it. Dr. Terry Melton, one of the most respected DNA scientists in the country, was going to conduct the test in Mitotyping Lab in Pennsylvania, the number one DNA laboratory in the country. Why would anyone not want to seek the truth? Especially when I paid for it.

The judge denied the state's motion to destroy the evidence but it still took a day-long hearing for us to win the petition to have the testing done. After the state sent the hair samples to the laboratory my attorneys received a call from Dr. Melton asking us what we wanted her to do. Of course, our response was to test the two hairs. But there was a problem with that. What none of us knew, because no one on the defense ever examined the hair evidence, was that there were a total of five to six microscopic slides. Each slide contained bunches of hair. Not a single slide had a label and the hairs were not even laid out straight. The laboratory had no idea which two hairs were the ones in question.

To test the entire number of hairs totaled around $80,000 and then to what point? Where did they come from? Which two hairs were the two used to convict me in the first place? At trial, assertive testimony inferred the recovery of two hairs from the crime scene, not multiple ones, and the prosecution's mantra was that those two hairs were a conclusive match to me.

At that point, we filed a Freedom of Information Act request with the FBI. We requested their file on my case, along with Agent Malone's notes, which should have directed us to which two hairs to test. It took over a year before we received a response. While my file did in fact exist, it wasn't in its storage place, and therefore unavailable. As such, the FBI denied my Freedom of Information Act. I had the option to appeal that decision if I chose to. Without that file or any indication of which hairs to test, my attorneys told the laboratory to return the slides and we withdrew our petition from the court.

It was at this point that I hit my lowest moment in my legal battle to prove my innocence and regain my freedom. My law firm, Ropes & Gray, was with me for almost twenty years at this point. They represented me pro bono the entire time, expending countless resources and billable hours. After the denial of the Freedom Of Information Act request, they contacted me to inform me that they pursued every avenue and exhausted all possible appeals. At this time they would withdraw from my case. That was soul-crushing news. For the first time I started questioning my hope, my drive, and the path I embarked on to lead a positive and productive life.

Several years went by in a bit of a blur, almost out of focus. I was no longer with representation, existing and going through the motions of prison life without any real direction. Then, in 2009, I read about a new law that our governor enacted, called the Writ of Actual Innocence. This law didn't require DNA evidence but rather focused on the totality of the evidence. For the first time, this law would allow an appeal to present evidence as a whole, rather than having to defend each individual allegation. For example, I could present a glass with wine in it and that would stand alone. However, if I added in a plate of food, silverware, a fancy table, and candlelight then that glass of wine now was part of a dinner setting, not a single glass of wine.

I reached out to Ropes & Gray and brought this new law to their attention. I didn't wait a week before a letter came from my attorney, stating the firm looked into it. If I was willing to have them come back on the case, they would undertake that petition on my behalf. I can't remember a time I rushed to grab a phone faster to say yes. My attorneys spent over a year researching for that writ and reviewing similar laws in other states. They prepared and filed a seventy-six-page writ on my behalf and in the spring of 2012 we were back in court.

The state's attorney could not resist expressing his displeasure to the court over my constant appeals. In an interview on public television, Cassilly discussed my case along with his displeasure with the fact that I refused to go away. He hated that I appealed a great deal. This time he complained to the court that I had the chance to DNA test the hairs but did not. Since we returned the hairs when we were unable to conduct the testing, the court was in the dark as to the reason why. My lawyers responded to Cassilly's complaints. They explained to the judge why the test was unable to proceed. The judge decided to suspend the hearing on the Writ of Actual Innocence and instructed the state to test those hairs.

For the rest of the summer, I waited on edge for the completion of the testing. We found out that the state's attorney was having DNA tested from every article of clothing associated with me, but for some odd reason, Cassilly was not testing the hairs as instructed. Every so often, the judge weighed in to ask how it was proceeding. The state responded each time that it was "in process," but they provided no details on the specifics of what Cassilly was testing. By fall, the state's attorney contacted my law firm and stated that the testing was complete and he was ready to proceed with the hearing – without any hair tests or results.

As my legal team prepared to finish this proceeding without the benefit of DNA testing on the hairs, a call came into the firm out of the blue. Spencer Hsu, a Washington Post reporter, was working on an exposé about the FBI's Hair Examination Lab. Of additional interest to him was the FBI agent who testified in my case, Agent Michael Malone. A whistleblower from the FBI crime lab came forward, and things surrounding my case were about to take a turn.

# CHAPTER 11

We learned that after the Oklahoma City bombing case in 1995, a whistleblower came out of the FBI laboratory. Dr. Frederick Whitehurst made numerous allegations about policies, procedures, and culture inside the Lab. They included failure to follow best practices, exertion of undue pressure and influence to direct findings, and that examiners "improperly testified outside their expertise, presented insupportable conclusions, perjured themselves, fabricated evidence, and failed to floor appropriate procedures." This resulted in a very lengthy and intensive investigation by the Office of the Inspector General (OIG) which issued a 517-page report in April 1997. In that report, they found several of Dr. Whitehurst's allegations to be true and flagged 13 agents. Specific to my case, their findings singled out senior FBI hair analyst Michael Malone's work. The report concluded that Malone consistently misrepresented evidence and testified outside of his area of expertise. We were aware of this report and retained a copy of it. It confirmed our opinion of Agent Malone and the testimony he gave at my trial, but by itself, it wasn't enough to utilize on any collateral appeal attack. My defense team felt we hadn't gained anything by it alone, and the FBI didn't begin using DNA testing in criminal cases until 1988.

When Spencer Hsu made contact with my law firm, their first response was no comment. Because we were still in the middle of a court proceeding we couldn't discuss the case with him. Hsu told them the specifics of what he was working on. As part of his research for the article, he obtained my FBI file, as well as those of other cases where FBI agent Malone testified. This was the same file we failed to obtain almost ten years earlier. When Spencer shared its contents we experienced an 'Ah-ha' moment, as it revealed why the state tried to destroy the hair evidence back in 2003 and why it hid that file.

While the OIG's investigation and report of the FBI lab were (and remains) a public document, what no one was aware of up to that moment was this. After the issuing of the OIG report, the FBI developed a Criminal Division Task Force in 1996. The Task Force conducted their own internal review and investigation. They hired outside forensic scientists to come in and review every case that involved FBI agent Malone, including mine. Of particular importance to the FBI task force report were the following:

The Task Force found that 96% of Malone cases were "problematic" in one or more areas. The most significant, recurring problems with his work were:

1. Unscientific and "outlandish" testimony that hair could belong to a single person to the exclusion of all others in the world.
2. Testimony on the statistical probability of a hair match based solely on microscopic analysis.
3. Conclusions were unclear and unsupported.
4. Testimony included analysis that was not documented in his bench notes.

In my FBI file was a copy of the Task Force report. They concluded that Agent Malone testified falsely in my case and went so far as to question whether Malone conducted the microscopic tests himself. Also, Malone testified in both of my trials that hair must have a minimum of 15 characteristics for comparison. Not only did the independent evaluator state that this opinion has no scientific basis, but the FBI lab's own manual for hair analysis (1977) also stated,

*"It is pointed out that hairs do not possess a sufficient number of unique microscopic characteristics to be positively identified as having originated from a particular person to the exclusion of all others."*

In addition to this document in my FBI file, there was a letter from the task force to State's Attorney Joseph Cassilly, dated nearly a decade prior, informing him there may be a problem with the hair evidence in my case and that he might want to notify either the defendant or his attorneys. He never did either.

While I sat reeling from this, my attorneys submitted the newfound information. In a motion for a new hearing, my team argued that Cassilly,

> "...*mischaracterized the results of an internal FBI investigation into Agent Malone's testimony in this case, falsely claiming that the independent analysis by the FBI "concluded that his testimony in this case was appropriate, that he did not overstate the case"* (Tr. of Br'g for Writ of Actual Innocence, March 30, 2011, at 46 ("Tr."))."

Hsu also contacted State's Attorney Cassilly for his response to the article. Once aware that this story would soon break in the Washington Post, Cassilly returned to the FBI for help. Suddenly, the FBI alleged they knew which two hairs to test. They informed us that they were going to test the hairs themselves, in their lab, and that their test would consume the samples. Of course, this made me paranoid and panicked. I pleaded with my attorneys to get the hairs sent to our lab for testing. They informed me that wasn't possible. Since the court instructed the state to conduct the testing, the state got the option to pick the lab. My legal team attempted to reassure me by telling me that the FBI testing would be peer-reviewed, meaning other scientists would watch. I wasn't convinced. How could I be? This was the same organization whose own agent's false testimony was key to the prosecution obtaining my conviction. Left with no choice, we waited.

Days and weeks went by and we fast approached our hearing date. I tried to stay focused on work and my programming efforts but I was too stressed and anxious to focus. Then, two days prior to the hearing, I heard that my attorneys needed me to call them as soon as possible. I went into the recreation hall where the inmate access phones were and called my attorney, Michael Laufert. In normal conversations and discussions with my attorneys, they are very professional and matter-of-fact. But that night, when Michael answered the phone, his impassioned voice was loud and clear. He didn't mince words and went straight to the point, "John. They're not your hairs."

Even when I learned my mother passed I held my emotions in check. In prison, emotions aren't allowed. At that moment, I couldn't hold it in. I sat in the day room area, with at least fifty other inmates present, on a pay phone mounted on the wall, and my eyes started leaking. I turned my face toward the wall in an attempt to regain my composure. It took over thirty-one years for the truth to come out. I couldn't talk. My emotions were everywhere. I remember telling my attorney that's all I ever wanted, that validation of truth. I didn't dare dream that I might see myself released. At that moment, the revelation of the truth was everything, but it was bittersweet.

My thoughts turned to my mom who believed in my innocence and stood by me the whole way. She was no longer alive to hear the news or witness this validation. My life hung in the precarious balance of a strand of hair. I swore then, and now, that her passing gained me an angel in Heaven who helped this happen. The long, twisted journey that brought us to this moment of truth was miraculous and I knew my guardian angel was guiding its course.

The selfish, ego-driven mentality of the state's attorney stole the truth from my mother as much as it stole the truth from me. Cassilly was the longest-serving State's attorney in Maryland history, retiring after thirty-seven years. He tried my case at a time in his career when he was the assistant state's attorney. With the publicity and resume of putting me on death row, he went on to run against his former boss and secure the position for

I was ignorant about the justice system in general. I held the belief that innocent people didn't get convicted and I supposed that it would get sorted out in the trial. In the beginning, I harbored no real resentment towards Cassilly. I felt he was doing his job, that it wasn't personal. That changed for me when Kanaras went on trial after me. From reading the local newspaper, my defense team and I would learn of four exculpatory witnesses that Cassilly used against Kanaras but never revealed to us. Each of these witnesses disputed Kanaras' claims that he sold me the gun. They each illustrated his desperation for money and addiction to drugs, contrary to his testimony. These witnesses included an undercover narcotics agent and two acquaintances. We filed a Brady violation at that time for this, but it was never ruled on since I won a new trial on other grounds.

That was the first reveal of the lengths that Cassilly would go to in securing my conviction with no regard to truth, ethics, or justice. The litany of his violations would continue as he made secret deals with Kanaras for his testimony, including not revealing he visited him in prison to discuss those deals. Cassilly appeared in court on Kanaras' behalf and took the stand to support his efforts to be released. After serving twenty-seven years, Kanaras was released in 2008.

The ultimate betrayal to me was his failure to disclose the FBI's information when they notified him in 1999. Instead of joining in the pursuit of justice and truth, he covered it up, going so far as to thwart our efforts to DNA test the hair samples in 2003.

His arrogance and boldness were astounding knowing what I know now, especially looking back at his request to destroy the evidence so testing could never occur. This cover up cost me an additional, unnecessary 14 years of incarceration. During that time I would hit my lowest points. In 1999, I would hit a depth of depression and despair that found me contemplating suicidal thoughts. In 2005, I would find myself without attorneys and questioning myself and my strength anew as to whether I should keep going forward. In 2009, I lost my mother to a heart attack. The opportunity to validate her belief in me or prove myself as the son she dreamed I would be was lost. Many times I found myself questioning what if? What if I made it home in '99 to be with her? Would it have prolonged her life or removed the stress that resulted in that heart attack? What would it have looked like for my non-existent relationship with my father if she were still alive? Would I have been able to repair that and have the opportunity to redeem myself? So many what-ifs, so many unresolved hamster wheels left forever in my head.

My legal team and I returned to that hearing now, armed with the truth and DNA results. Cassilly confronted us with arrogance, denial, and more outright lies. It's not uncommon for evidence like this to come out years or decades later. I expected the attorneys would work together to do the right thing. The one thing Cassilly proved interested in was denying any wrongdoing and defending himself.

He tried to argue that the test results and hair evidence meant nothing and that I was plain guilty. He outright lied to the court claiming he sent notifications to the Innocence Project and the public defender's office back in 1999. Both entities stated that this claim wasn't true. In fact, the public defender's office stopped representing me when David Stewart took over my case in 1986 and I wasn't associated with the Innocence Project until 2003. Cassilly was aware and quite familiar that attorneys from Ropes & Gray took me on as a client in 1988. Furthermore, he could not produce or provide any proof of these notifications to the court.

I can remember the vivid details of that day. The judge wore the best poker face I have ever seen. Cassilly was in full dramatic mode, like a soap opera actor, he held his head upright without lifting it high enough to meet the judge's eyes. While I could not get a sense of what the judge thought, the look on his clerk's face and the body language she gave Cassilly were priceless. She couldn't keep the incredulity from her expression. She glanced at him in unabashed amazement at each of his ridiculous explanations and arguments. Once I noticed, I watched her expressions more than anything else that day.

After a full day of argument in court, the judge announced he was going to take it under advisement and issue his ruling at a later date. Of course, I was anxious about my past experience when it took three and a half years to get a ruling. One of the local reporters covering the hearing spoke with the court clerk and reported that the judge would rule in the next thirty to sixty days. In about a month, my attorneys informed me that they received the judge's ruling. They told me it was several pages long but read me the conclusion.

*The Writ of Actual Innocence is hereby granted, convictions reversed, sentences rescinded and the case remanded to the State for further proceedings.*

Another overwhelming, emotional moment. I let myself cry. This wasn't real. I never allowed myself to see that far forward, toward the possibility of getting out. Freedom was always the goal but also an illusion. Now it loomed as a potential reality and I wasn't sure how to react. Then my attorney explained that it was now in the hands of the same state's attorney who orchestrated my fate in the legal system from the start. That boggled my mind and was yet another example of how screwed up the legal system is. Because of what our team saw from him over the years, it was imminent that he would retry me for the third time. My attorney advised our next step would be filing for a bail review. I asked him how much he thought it would be. He commented that in a case similar to mine the bail was set at $100,000. My heart stopped. He might as well have said a million dollars. I didn't have that kind of money or financial support. Yet another obstacle on this journey. My elation evaporated.

# CHAPTER 12

Ropes & Gray filed for a bail hearing, which was not scheduled for another seventy-six days from the ruling. For seventy-six days I remained in a maximum-security prison with no conviction or sentence. I was in pretrial status. That meant I should have transferred back to the Harford County Detention Center. Non-convicted individuals cannot stay in the general population of any state prison, let alone maximum-security.

Because the bail hearing was being held in Frederick County, authorities transferred me to the regional maximum-security prison for that area the day before. The state prison system runs a transportation unit for proceedings like this and when they're in different segments of the state they will transfer inmates in advance. It ensured I was already in the area and available. When an individual goes into another prison under transportation they're not allowed anything other than the clothes on their back and their legal papers. That's it. Not even an ink pen, pencil, or a book to read. They're put in an isolation cell the day before and an additional night because they don't transfer inmates back to their originating prison until the day after their court appearance.

The bail hearing lasted about an hour. I went into it with my thoughts consumed over how to put together a $100,000 bail. I had very little money and spoke with friends who expressed their willingness to help. One, in particular, Laura Robinson, connected me with a bondsman. I met Laura through the Jaycees in the '90s. At that time she was a nurse. Since then she changed her career path, becoming one of the most prominent defense attorneys in Anne Arundel County and now a District Court Judge. She referred me to a bondsman who worked with several of her clients.

With these resources in place, it seemed I did everything in my power to make this a realistic possibility; that is until I stood before the court for the decision. The judge set my bail at $500,000 cash. It was another one of several moments in my life where news handed to me felt like a sledgehammer to the gut. It left me rocking back and forth on my heels with nary a breeze in the room.

Taken back to the isolation cell in the maximum-security prison, I spent the next 24 hours with my thoughts on overdrive trying to figure out how to raise half a million dollars. That day for lunch they served tomato soup. Since I wasn't allowed to have a pen or a pencil, I took the end of my spork and dipped it into the soup for ink. I destroyed several of my legal documents with tomato soup ink while trying to calculate numbers and formulas to reach that $500,000 mark.

The next day I returned to my originating prison and as soon as I could, I grabbed a phone to connect with my attorneys. Their news stopped me cold before I could get into any of my impossible calculations. My attorney said, "John, you're coming home today," as if this kind of thing happened all the time. Friends made it happen through the bail bondsman that Laura arranged. The bondsman was at that very moment in the Frederick courthouse finalizing the documents.

I called my best friend, John Jones, who went home four months earlier and shared the news. His excitement at the news got me excited. Repeating it out loud to someone else made it real for me. He told me a group of friends was going to the Kem concert that night and there was a ticket for me to go as well. Kem is one of my favorite R&B artists and that made me more excited.

I went back to my cell and started going through my property. I packed personal photos, letters, and legal work. It was everything I would take with me and then made arrangements to leave my TV, radio, and everything else to friends on the tier. I waited and waited for the tier officer to call my name. When someone is leaving the tier, officers holler out their name, followed by "Bag and baggage." That means to grab their belongings and report to the desk for further instructions. That call never came.

It is rare for an inmate to bail out of state prison. That's something that typically occurs in county jails and detention centers. The bondsman completed the necessary paperwork well before 3 p.m. and transmitted it to the appropriate department at prison headquarters. However, the woman on the receiving end didn't know what to do with it. Since it was a Friday afternoon, she left the paperwork on a desk when she went home for the weekend. Somehow, I managed to fulfill the requirements and pay $500,000 bail, in cash, and this was the result.

At this point, the prison case management department was aware my bail was paid. Now they were concerned for my safety in the prison as a non-convicted, non-sentenced person, and were contemplating locking me in isolation. I argued that they weren't worried about that for the past seventy-six days and that I'd be fine. I offered to sign waivers, whatever it took because the last thing I needed was to be in lockdown and isolated from phone communication. There was no issue over my safety after thirty-two years of incarceration. My fellow convicts were happy for me.

Somehow I made it through one of the longest weekends of my life. Of course, I was on the phone with my attorneys as soon as possible on Monday morning. When I reached Ryan Malone at my attorney's office, he jumped into action. He called administrators at the Department of Public Safety & Correctional Services multiple times. It was about 1 p.m. when I was called down to the Traffic Office and the paperwork processing me out began. When that was complete, it was the assistant warden who personally walked me out to the front where my sister was waiting to pick me up. Monday, July 22, 2013, my freedom day.

I walked out that afternoon to a beautiful summer day. The sun seemed brighter and the air seemed different as well. It was difficult for my eyes to focus at first. Everything was hazy. I was on sensory overload and I couldn't walk. My sister and I got into her car and stopped for gas. I stepped out of the car and stood there looking around, drinking a Mountain Dew as if I were drinking in life itself.

I asked to use my sister's phone and called the bondsman. My voice was full of excitement as I told him "I'm out." His unfazed response was "Of course you are, I posted your bail." It seems logical to me now, but at that moment I wasn't sure what to do. I asked him if I needed to report to him, let him take my picture, or sign something. He told me that because I was friends with Laura and her husband, John, I was cool with him. Then he told me, "Go live your best life."

In the distance from the gas station, I could see the MCE logo on a building. I worked for them inside for the past twenty years, so I knew the headquarters was somewhere close. I told my sister that I wanted to make a quick pit stop at the plant. I wanted to say goodbyes and express my appreciation for the opportunities MCE afforded me. Using her phone, I called my regional manager and he said he'd be right over to meet me. He gave me a tour of the place and I met in person people I knew for years by phone. It seemed like the right thing to do at the time for closure and I'm glad I did it.

From there I went to my sister's house for a cookout with her and her husband, Lee. It felt good to relax outside and play with the dogs. It felt good to have grass under my bare feet and to experience trees and the outdoors. To go barefoot was a treat. In prison, we wore shoes to the shower and then changed into shower shoes. It's a security measure of sorts, to stay prepared with shoes on and laced up.

Of course, the whole ride home I monopolized my sister's cell phone calling everyone on my list to let them know I was free. My sister decided at that point, if she was ever to get her phone back, she would need to take me to get one for myself as soon as possible. That afternoon she took me to purchase my first phone. After that, it was time to report to the transition house and check-in.

# CHAPTER 13

As part of the conditions of my bail release, I resided at the Patrick Allison House in Baltimore, a transitional house with an eight-bed capacity for returning citizens. It's where my best friend, John Jones, also stayed. The program at the house lasts six months to a year before residents transition out. It's located in a very nice area of Baltimore called Mount Vernon with a large row home that used to be the pastor's manse of the Presbyterian Church located next door. There were five bedrooms, three of which were double occupancy. None of the bedroom doors had locks. Residents shared the common areas of the kitchen, living room, and dining room. There was a curfew at night and a requirement that residents sign out with their destination(s) any time they left the house and sign back in upon returning. There were mandatory, weekly house meetings as well as mandatory AA/NA meetings. Another expectation for residents required them to work at or enroll in the Project SERVE program, a partnership the House shared with Living

Classrooms Foundation. It wasn't complete freedom but it was still a step up from a six-by-nine prison cell.

I enrolled in the Project SERVE program at Living Classrooms Foundation a week after my return. The program's design was a rapid attachment to work concept that allows a returned citizen to earn money while receiving full wraparound case management services. There were two main work components of the program which consisted of either cleaning vacant city-owned properties or cleaning the promenade at the Inner Harbor, which was the city's main tourist attraction. I wasn't assigned to either but instead given a desk job and title. I took on the roles of client advocate and event organizer, in which I acted as a conduit between the other participants and their case managers. In addition, my job required me to arrange a monthly calendar of workshops and other occasions.

This was a minimum-wage job but it was something. I learned how to get about town using the metro, which was a brand new experience. For me, Baltimore was scary and overwhelming. I never feared walking the yards of the toughest prisons in the state, but Baltimore was a whole different story. The murder rate skyrocketed the summer I came home and apathy among the city youth was unmistakable. The week before I came into the house there was a double murder at an establishment right on the corner of my block. For a long time, I didn't venture out of my immediate surroundings to explore the neighborhood. I went to work every day and when I got home, I either sat on the front stoop of the house or walked over to the neighboring park and sat there. I stayed in at night. No partying for me. Another one of the conditions of my bail was no alcohol or drugs. I wasn't interested in either. I focused on figuring out my life. I saved every penny I earned and, within a year, paid back the friends who helped put up the money for my bail.

Nothing about my return was easy or handed to me. Despite a wonderful network of associates, real friends and family weren't part of the equation. The thing about any relationship when it comes to incarceration, whether it's romantic or platonic, is that they rarely last. The minute a person gets locked up, they learn that their relationships weren't what they thought they were. People tend to disassociate. Even lifelong childhood friends disappear into the wind. It's understandable for a lot of reasons, notably when a person gets locked up at a young age as I did. Hell, if I couldn't even process incarceration at eighteen years old, how could I expect my friends to? They soon faded away as well, out of sight, out of mind. I saw a few marriages last the duration of incarceration, but I can't begin to imagine how hard that was to maintain. If convicts didn't have a pre-existing romantic relationship, the odds of finding one while incarcerated were about non-existent. While I dated and had girlfriends while locked up, I'm sure I didn't know squat about relationships. I didn't have a lot of support, but the one person I thought I could count on was Lynn. We talked on the phone almost every day after my release. I was in love with her for the past twenty-five years and she was my entire world. She moved several years prior back to her home state of Georgia. At the time of my release, she was in Germany on business. We made plans for her to come to Maryland in August for my birthday. One afternoon on the phone I felt the need to ask her if she ever married. I don't know why, but something instinctual made me do it. There was a long, silent pause. She said she would rather talk about it when she came up in August. I stopped dead in my tracks, and that dreadful feeling I used to get waiting for a court ruling began to rise. My heart raced as I pressed her for an answer.

When she said, "Yes, I am married," I couldn't breathe. I felt like the same sledgehammer that kicked my ass my entire adult life hit me in the stomach anew. I pressed further, asking for how long. She replied for the past 10 years. Lynn explained that she never stopped loving me, but she gave up the belief that I would ever get released. She met someone, fell in love, and got married. She still loved me and didn't want to lose me, which is why she chose not to tell me. I couldn't hear her. My mind raced over the events of the past 10 years. My parents loved her. She attended my parent's 50th wedding anniversary party and represented us as a couple. Twenty-five years of visits, letters, and phone calls flashed through my mind. While I struggled to figure out my return to the world, in that one phone call I lost my closest confidante. It rocked my world.

I took a few days to absorb everything and accepted her explanation. We saw each other once a month over the next several months but it didn't work out as a romantic relationship. I will always value and appreciate her presence in my life for those difficult twenty-five years. She was my light, my hope, and my inspiration to keep moving forward even on my darkest days. I am forever grateful. We are still friends to this day and she will always hold a piece of my heart.

Relationships are tough at best, but I didn't know how to date. I felt like I wasn't bringing anything to the table. My past always needed explaining. I was fifty years old, making minimum wage. I didn't own a car or a house and there was a prosecutor intent on sending me straight back to prison for life. What woman could resist?

I'm a firm believer in listening to the universe. It reveals what we're meant to know at the right time. I did meet another fantastic lady, a doctor named Hillary. While I initially resisted, she turned to me at one point after a few months and stated, "You know we're in a relationship, right?" She loves to tell the story of how I endlessly pursued her to go out with me. In reality, I was hesitant about evolving into a relationship. I didn't feel I brought anything to the table. Little did I know that I needed her support, advice, and guidance. I needed to feel that I could be a better man and set my sights higher. As much as I needed to focus on the upcoming trial, I also needed to believe I had a future. She was an amazing and supportive partner who helped ensure my reintegration succeeded.

Another part of my problem with my return to society was how I presented myself. Decades of surviving alone and not revealing emotion created the impression that I was okay, that I had my shit together. In reality, I was completely lost. The world passed me by during my incarceration and now I was a fish out of water. I didn't understand the technology and the pace of life. Choices, while a welcome opportunity, caused me serious anxiety. I didn't know how to order food in a restaurant, how to shop for appropriate clothing, or how automatic toilets and hand washing stations worked. I remember a conversation with a coworker at our job one day. He was the mentoring coordinator for Living Classrooms and his role was to assign and connect mentors for the participants in Project SERVE. His desk was next to mine and one day I asked him why he didn't assign me a mentor. He seemed surprised by the question and said, "I didn't think you needed one." I tried to present myself with confidence, but it worked against me to the point that people rarely thought about where I came from and what I went through. Well, after thirty-two years and fifty-five days, there were quite a few things I could have used help with. Because of my background in graphics, the mentoring coordinator suggested a thirty-two-year-old unemployed graphics artist who might be a good match for me. I sort of chuckled at that and politely declined. I wasn't sure who would have been the mentor in that relationship.

On the outside, it appeared that my reentry was going well. I hid the enormous difficulty of adapting to my new life. It was hard adapting to societal norms. My first impression was how self-absorbed people seemed to have become. It was strange for me to see people with their white earbuds in their ears and faces buried in their phones as they walked through the city, oblivious to their surroundings and their community. One summer afternoon, I returned from work and lay on my bed on the third floor of the transitional home. My window was open and rain started to fall when I heard a commotion coming from the street. When I looked out I saw a struggle going on between a woman and a man. The woman was crying out for help. I jumped up from the bed and dashed down three flights of stairs into the street, shoeless and shirtless. The man was slinging the woman around by the shoulder strap of her purse as she hung on with all her might. As I slammed the door open and raced toward them, he saw me coming and took off running without the purse. A neighbor driving past stopped and together we walked the woman over to her house to wait for her husband and the local authorities. While we caught our breath, I noticed an older gentleman sitting on the stoop feet away. He watched the entire incident unfold without offering any help. I left the woman at her neighbor's place when the authorities arrived. I noticed my foot bleeding from stepping on glass. After the incident, some of my friends chastised me for getting involved. "What if he had a knife or a gun?"

My response was, "What if it was your sister or your mother?"

I left Project SERVE after three months and went to work for another local non-profit, Second Chance. Second Chance is a social enterprise that deconstructs buildings and homes, salvages usable materials, and makes those, along with other donated items, available for sale to the public. They hired me to observe and review the receiving department. After a few weeks, they named me department manager. Once that department returned to some semblance of order Second Chance offered me an additional position as a sales manager for deconstruction sales. There I managed a 1.5 million dollar portfolio worth of properties. I had a salary, drove a company car, and considered that my life was going to work out. The founder and President, Mark Foster, took me under his wing and provided mentorship and a friendship that remains to this day.

I worked for Second Chance for a little over a year when Living Classrooms reentered the picture. I was working on a separate project with them to create an Entrepreneurship Incubator for returning citizens to create their own businesses when the Living Classrooms' president asked me to apply for an open position as workforce director for their Baltimore programs. I wouldn't have given that a second thought. I didn't imagine that I'd have a chance at a position like that as I was on bail, facing a murder trial and possible re-incarceration for life. Who would want to risk that investment in me? But he convinced me to do it. This led to an interview from which they hired me. I oversaw Living Classrooms' adult workforce and job training efforts for Baltimore. They promoted me to senior staff in the Foundation with a direct staff of almost 20 employees, a budget of $3.5 million, 3 physical buildings to manage, plus we worked with over 1,000 people a year. Project SERVE, the very program I came through after my release, was now under my portfolio.

At first, it was a little overwhelming. There was a lot to learn. I inherited a 1.2 million dollar federal grant that was improperly managed and the workforce department that I inherited was off the rails. However, within the first eight months under my leadership, I turned it around. The staff grew into a productive team and our services expanded. My personal network grew and I came to be one of the most recognizable faces of the Living Classrooms Foundation. I found myself serving on the Governor's Task Force, the leadership team for the mayor, and I joined board positions for several other non-profits throughout Baltimore City. It seemed I found my passion and I was good at it.

# CHAPTER 14

Despite my successful career trajectory and extensive community service work, Joseph Cassilly was quick to dispel and destroy any illusion of freedom. The preparations for the upcoming trial were well underway and he was making no secret of his desire to see me return to prison. Juggling my attempts to start a career and lead a normal, healthy life while faced with the possibility of going back to prison for the rest of my life created a lot of stress and pressure. I wasn't free in the truest sense of the word. All I did was trade up for a larger prison cell.

Because I was on bail, I fell under the authority of the department of parole and probation. They assigned a parole and probation officer to me, who in my case functioned as a pretrial officer. I had a single, in-person meeting with her which went so well that for the next few months she asked me to report via kiosk and then not report at all. Later she told me to contact her by email to obtain travel permits if I left the state. We became colleagues and friends. She referred her clients to Project SERVE and attended our annual first Monday empowerment group banquet. This was the normal interaction within the network I built. In my professional life, no one cared that I was on bail or facing trial. It seemed that the work I did was enough.

I presented a normal façade because my role as director required me to meet deadlines with first-class deliverables. The staff counted on me and the people I reported to trusted me. Additionally, the community I cared for expected me to deliver and often pull off miracles for their lives. I worked sixty-plus hour weeks trying to fulfill everyone's expectations. The stress and anxiety built inside me with the ever-looming cloud of the upcoming trial.

My attorneys, led by senior partner Chong Park, prepared to take this to a third trial and devoted the entire resources of the firm to this effort. Chong is the epitome of perseverance and dedication. He does Iron Man triathlons for fun! He is tenacious and honorable. I couldn't say how many associates, summer interns, and other support staff applied countless hours of work and energy on my behalf. Ropes & Gray has quantified that there were over 120 attorneys that put work into my case over three decades. Two senior partners oversaw my case, Chong and Alex Rene'. For the first time since this ordeal began, brilliant and competent attorneys represented me. However, the trial date never seemed to materialize. I was out for about three years before the state's attorney sent a plea offer to my lawyer. In short, it said if I plead guilty to two counts of murder, the case would close. It would be time served and I would not return to prison.

Cassilly gave me a month to consider it. He was so convinced that I would take the offer that he announced his retirement.

I spent a lot of sleepless nights over it. I hated to give any real thought to taking a deal, but the guarantee of ending this persecution without the threat of returning to prison with a life sentence was something I needed to consider. One thing I noticed more frequently was that no one cared about my innocence. People I met didn't question it. No one seemed to care that I was not fully exonerated. It gave me doubt about why I should care so much. Plus, I was still up against Cassilly.

I went to New York City and met Jenny Thompson, a friend of mine who moved there from Baltimore. She was adamant that I should not take the deal. Jenny was one of the few people in my life that risked giving an opinion. A big supporter and contributor to the Innocence Project, she expressed her opinion that I wouldn't be able to live with myself if I was not living in truth. I realized this was what I already thought. I believed whatever kept me alive and going forward that whole 32 years, 2 months, and 28 days was in jeopardy if I did not fight for the truth. I was afraid the little flame inside me would go out; that I wouldn't be me anymore. It came down to would I be able to look at myself in the mirror?

I went to my mother's grave and talked to her about it. Spending time there, I realized my truth. There was no way that I was ever going to say I was guilty of these crimes. I spent my whole adult life fighting to prove my innocence. I owed it to myself, my mother, and my family to stand behind that truth no matter the cost. I gave talks at colleges and universities throughout Maryland, New Jersey, San Diego, and London. I wasn't about to sell my soul for the expediency of his offer. When I said no to the deal, coincidence or not, Cassilly withdrew his retirement. In my mind, I believed he felt that his successor wouldn't prosecute me and that he was intent on protecting his legacy, image, and reputation.

After I turned down the deal, my attorneys put trial prep into high gear, but one issue created more stress for me. Neither of the senior partners felt that they were the right fit to be lead counsel. My trial was to be in Frederick County, MD, which was a bit of a white enclave with a definite racial bend. My two primary attorneys were African-American and Korean. We went on a search to bring in lead counsel which took me to Houston, Texas. There I met with Patricia Cummings who joined my legal team at Ropes & Gray. Patricia was part of the legal team who represented Michael Morton. A defendant in a highly publicized Texas case, Morton was convicted of murdering his wife. It took twenty-five years of fighting before he was exonerated. A DNA test cleared him and it proved someone else killed his wife. Like in my case, prosecutor misconduct was also in play. After his exoneration, the prosecutor in his case was found guilty of withholding exculpatory evidence. That prosecutor was the only one to ever spend time in jail for misconduct that led to a wrongful conviction. His sentence was ten days in jail, of which he served a total of four days. It paled in comparison to the quarter of a century Morton spent in prison for a crime he didn't commit.

Now the pressures of an upcoming trial were stronger than ever. Cassilly sent my attorneys a snide letter when presenting the plea deal where he said, "I don't have anything to lose {by going forward to trial} but what are you going to tell your client when they slap handcuffs on him in the courtroom and take him back to prison for the rest of his life?"

Because I turned down his generous offer, Cassilly decided he would do anything and everything to send me back to prison. There were things coming into our world that were very unsettling. We thought we knew everything there was to know about the case and the evidence they claimed to possess implicating me. In his blind intent to re-convict me, Cassilly threatened my defense with two new witnesses. We would have to address repressed memories from a witness who was a child at the time of the murders. He also added an officer from my initial security detail from the first trial. Cassilly claimed the officer would testify that I confessed to him during a break in the first trial. My case went on for over thirty-five years, which included two complete trials and countless appeals. Neither of these witnesses was mentioned during any of that time. It was obvious that Cassilly would continue to abuse the power of his office in order to pursue and convict me.

While this pressed forward, I still worked as the director of workforce development for the Living Classrooms Foundation. I grew the department and achieved a measure of success by creating new training programs and workforce partners. The true measure of success came from our participants' successes, those who transitioned back into society and gained livable income wage jobs, purchased cars and homes, and started families. Our recidivism rate fell below 14% and I was proud to be a part of those success stories. I took tours back into the prison system to visit the MCE sign plant where I worked, as well as other prison plants. My goal was to introduce people to the efforts incarcerated men and women underwent to better themselves and prepare for their eventual return to society. I wanted to weld together the services and efforts of those on the outside with what was taking place on the inside. I took judges, cabinet secretaries from the governor's office, community-based organizations working in re-entry, and Ray Lewis of the Baltimore Ravens on prison tours. Through the course of those efforts, I established a strong working relationship with the secretary of public safety and correctional services, the man who oversaw the entire Maryland prison system. We developed a strong mutual respect for one another even though his father was the Sheriff of Harford County in 1981 when I was first arrested. He supported my efforts in bringing re-entry resources into the prisons through opportunity fairs. But, it was difficult to carry the responsibilities I felt toward those citizens' needs while I balanced the myriad of pressures and concerns related to my future. I tried to keep my body and mind busy.

A few months before my scheduled trial, my attorneys received a phone call from Cassilly. He informed them that a high-level state government official reached out to him. This official questioned him about my case and talked to him in-depth about my work in the community. Cassilly expressed irritation and asked us how many more of these types of calls he should expect. We didn't know that this individual contacted him until he told us. This was the moment he asked my attorneys if I would consider taking an Alford Plea and requested they discuss it with me. The Alford Plea allowed me to maintain my innocence, with the recognition that there is potential evidence that might convict me. It is usually an offer made to an individual while they are still incarcerated. Through my observation of other cases where Alford pleas were offered, prosecutors tended to abuse this plea as a promise of immediate release versus a lengthy prison stay while awaiting a new trial.

This offer was one that required careful consideration for a number of reasons. I maintained a career, a professional network, and people who counted on me. There was an organization, Living Classrooms, that invested in me and gave me an incredible opportunity to make a difference and have an impact. All the while, they knew I was facing an uncertain future. On the other hand, there was the prosecutor, who already bent and/or broke every rule of law to gain a conviction. No one gave me an opinion on this, but family, friends, and support networks said they would respect whatever decision I made. I felt alone and isolated and never more uncertain in my life.

After a long period of contemplation, I took the Alford Plea. I can't point to a single reason, but I had trepidation about the prosecutor and the judge assigned to the trial. The judge, as we discovered, was the clerk for the judge in my original trial. She harbored substantial feelings towards me in that regard. I sensed there was no level playing field and that I wouldn't receive a fair trial.

I felt an obligation to the Living Classrooms Foundation, the organization that provided my employment opportunity at the time. I didn't want any negative publicity that a retrial could bring to overshadow their work in the city because I was an employee. I feared that win-lose-or-draw, a trial could have an adverse effect on my network and my ability to deliver the services and work that I do. When I walked into prison, I lost everything. Prison stripped everything away. The only thing left was my truth. Asking me to surrender, asking me to give up the fight, to give up on me, was the hardest hurdle to overcome. I weighed who I was at that point. In addition to my new career, I sat on the Governor's Task Force on Collateral Consequences. I participated or partnered with the Greater Baltimore Second Chance Coalition, the Baltimore City Police Re-entry Advisement Committee, and several other non-profit boards. For the first time in my adult life, an extensive network of folks, both professionally and personally, supported and respected me and my efforts. There could have been collateral consequences if we went to trial. I examined the bigger picture and thought about how a third trial would affect everyone and my relationships with them. It was the hardest decision of my life.

On December 7, 2017, I received my sentence under the Alford Plea, my personal day of infamy. The judge launched into a tirade as she accepted the deal and sentenced me. I stood there and took her vitriol. One of my attorneys turned to me when she finished and said that now he understood. He offered his apology for what I endured over the past three decades. Then he showed me his palm. He clenched his fists so tight during the judge's sermon, that there were fingernail imprints. It was to prevent himself from reacting to her scathing rhetoric. I left the courtroom that day and drove straight to Stone Harbor Beach in New Jersey. I needed to get away, decompress, and collect myself. I went straight to the beach and jumped into the ocean as I tried to cleanse my spirit. It was a cold day in December, but I needed to do it. As I got out of the water, it started snowing and ended up being the worst blizzard of the year.

I stayed on parole and probation until the end of 2017. It wasn't until January 1, 2018, that I was free and clear of the criminal justice system. Before that, I felt like I had one foot in, one foot out, and that one foot was on a banana peel. My conviction, my time inside, my trials, and my record stymied everything. It blocked healthy relationships in my personal life and it prevented my ability to move up in my employment. It took away a lifetime of other opportunities.

I needed to reconsider how I envisioned my future. In the past, I lived in *carpe diem* mode because my future was uncertain. Now that the threat of returning to prison no longer loomed, I considered what my life looked like. It was difficult to move on, even harder to continue going out and giving talks. I felt fake like I sold out my truth. The light inside me dimmed.

# CHAPTER 15

To be honest, I never reconciled taking the Alford plea. I felt like I sold a piece of my soul. There are moments in life when it's necessary to make a tough decision. Once it's made, then you have to live with it. That's what I did. There were things that I gave up with that deal that I will never get back. Part of which will always be that there will be people who will question my guilt or innocence. I decided to file a grievance against Cassilly with the Attorney Grievance Commission (AGC) of Maryland. The AGC is the watchdog of the state's judicial system, meaning they oversee and ensure that lawyers are fulfilling their obligations, ethically practicing law, and upholding the rules of professional conduct of attorneys.

I kept my expectations low. I felt the AGC would protect their own, especially someone elected for as long as Cassilly. He was the longest-serving prosecutor in Maryland's history and was at one time the president of the state's attorneys Trial Association. He certainly gained standing in the community. I was under no false illusion that the AGC would take the case, let alone do anything about it. To date, only 4% of prosecutors in the United States involved in wrongful conviction cases tainted by prosecutorial misconduct have faced any kind of personal or professional discipline, according to the National Registry of Exonerations. Just a small handful of these prosecutors faced serious disciplinary action, such as disbarment from the practice of law, as opposed to a brief suspension or reprimand by the state bar. To my surprise and gratitude, the AGC took on my case in a very serious manner. They investigated for about a year, then on May 21, 2019, they sent an investigator to speak with me. The investigator, who was a retired Baltimore City homicide detective, made it very clear in the initial interview that he didn't like what he discovered through his research. Here was a guy involved in hundreds of homicide cases from the other side of the coin, and he seemed offended by what Cassilly did in my case.

The reason my case proceeded in this manner was that everything was documented clearly through the years. It's not my word versus his. The letters, court documents, and transcripts are available. These files include what Cassilly misrepresented to the court, the misleading testimony, trying to have evidence destroyed, and what he covered up.

When the AGC completed their investigation, they filed a statement of charges against Joseph Cassilly. Filing charges against a state's attorney is almost unheard of anywhere in this country. The charges were based on ethical and code of professional conduct violations. An interesting reflection on Cassilly's character is that Bar Counsel added a charge of their own for Cassilly refusing to provide his statement under oath. No "normal" witness can testify or be deposed without taking the oath. Cassilly felt that he was the exception.

Once the Attorney Grievance Commission files charges, the next step is a peer review hearing. This is where the AGC composes a panel consisting of five individuals, including four attorneys and one public member, to hear testimony and review evidence regarding the statement of charges. This hearing took place on February 12th, 2020, at a law firm in Harford County, a five-minute drive from the church where my parents are buried. I went out before the hearing that morning and visited their graves.

The hearing started at 10 a.m. in a tiny board room that barely accommodated the twelve of us. For the first time in the entire forty-year saga, we sat close enough to look each other in the eye. My attorney, Rachel Endick, was present but not permitted in the actual hearing. She remained in an adjoining room if there came a need to consult with her.

The unfortunate physical dynamics of the room enhanced the palpable vibe that permeated the air. In the past, I chose to ignore Cassilly and not allow him space in my head or feelings. On that day we were too close in proximity. I already felt emotional from visiting my parents' grave site which crystallized the cost of what he did to me. My mother didn't live long enough to see the truth revealed or welcome me home in 2013. My father was in the beginning stages of dementia and Alzheimer's by the time I returned. It's probable he never comprehended my release. Now, I sat across from the individual who exacted that cost. He was the primary person responsible for my parents' lost chance to see me freed.

The animosity and disrespect shown toward me by Cassilly and his attorney during that hearing were relentless. They objected to everything I said or made snide remarks and comments. Their body language conveyed deep contempt. I sat still and listened as they both talked over each other, spewing lies and misrepresenting the facts to the panel. The Bar Counsel did a good job of presenting my case. They allowed Cassilly and his lawyer to talk themselves into a deeper hole. After four hours of enduring this, I asked to speak. Of course, Cassilly and his attorney both objected. The panel foreperson counseled me to keep my comments respectful. I made a very brief statement, thanking Bar Counsel and the panel for their hard work, time, and attention to the review. I denied Cassilly's assertions that I filed these charges to be vindictive. My contention was that the outcome of the case had nothing to do with my personal situation. It was about correcting the abuse of the process, misuse of his power as a prosecutor, and reinstating faith in our justice system. A system, that as an inexperienced, 18-year-old kid, I trusted in, convinced that the truth would come out at my first trial. Instead, because of Cassilly's rampant misconduct, I talked to a tombstone that morning. Because of Cassilly's abuse and wrongdoing, I was sitting in this tiny conference room forty years later listening to his continuous falsehoods and misrepresentations. I thanked the group of participants for their hard work and requested to be excused from the remainder of the hearing. I couldn't stomach another minute of being in his presence, listening to more lies. They excused me and I left.

Outside, Rachel gave me a big hug and it took several minutes for my whole body to stop trembling and for me to compose myself enough to drive home. There was no reason to suppose anything would come of the hearing. It felt like this was his world, his turf, and the establishment would close ranks to protect their own.

Bar Counsel informed me the next day that the hearing continued for several hours after I left. Much to my surprise, they notified me that the panel found Cassilly in violation of each and every one of the charges. The panel then recommended a verbal reprimand, which Cassilly refused to accept. The next review was by the *en banc* panel of the Maryland Attorney Grievance Commission who decided if public charges should be placed next. They reviewed this at their next scheduled meeting and instructed Bar Counsel to go back to him and try to negotiate a verbal reprimand solution. That did not meet with any success. He outright refused to accept any decision of wrongdoing on his part. It then went back to the Maryland Attorney Grievance Commission and this time, on September 8, 2020, they filed a petition for disciplinary action against Cassilly. This meant a public trial in circuit court.

Cassilly's trial occurred on February 3-5, 2021 in front of Judge Barbara Howe. COVID-19 protocols required this to be conducted via video conference. As a witness, I wasn't allowed to listen in until after I testified. The hearing went on for three days and waiting was tough. Three days of listening to lies and misrepresentations. His lawyer made blatant attempts to influence the judge with name-dropping and politicking. On March 10, 2021, Judge Barbara Howe issued a twenty-six-page decision that found Cassilly guilty of all six charges including withholding exculpatory evidence, lying to the court, and other ethics violations. She stated that my team failed to establish a violation regarding the refusal to take the oath charge.

I cried the day I got that news. When I shared the news with my girlfriend, the second she hugged me the tears flowed. I held back my emotions for a lifetime and waited forty years for this. It came from somewhere deep inside me. I still can't find the words to describe what it's like to wait forty years for the truth to come out at last. It's not relatable. Who has to wait forty years for anything?

That wasn't the end of it. There was still an appeal for Cassilly to file. In Maryland, the sole entity that has the power to sanction an attorney is Maryland's highest court, the Maryland Court of Appeals. That hearing was held via video conference on September 9, 2021. For the umpteenth time I endured the regurgitation of lies. Cassilly's assertions that he'd done nothing wrong and somehow ended up a victim of the Black Lives Matter movement and an anti-police climate sickened me. It was so hard to sit through and listen to something that made zero sense. His actions, and the documentation of those actions, occurred throughout the case from 1981 until my Alford Plea. Neither of those movements or climates existed during that time. Cassilly had no substantial defense and refused to accept that he engaged in any wrongdoing.

October 22, 2021, I sat at my desk at work when an email came in from Tim Prudente, a writer for the Baltimore SUN newspaper. He requested comment on the Cassilly ruling. I was unaware there was a ruling. I jumped up from my desk, excited but not sure what was going on. I shouted to my boss and co-worker that a ruling was in as I raced outside to make phone calls. I tried calling my attorney, and when he didn't answer, I called Tim at the SUN. He wanted me to comment, but I told him that I didn't know what the ruling was. He informed me that in a unanimous decision, the Court of Appeals disbarred Cassilly. The next hour was a total blur. I tried calling my attorneys but none were answering. I called my girlfriend and my good friend and hero, Jason Flom. I couldn't get the words out and I didn't have any substantiating information. I called Tim again and asked where he saw the decision. He agreed to send me a copy of the court of appeals decision and asked that I respond back to him within an hour with my comment. I shared the court of appeals decision with my attorneys. We each read through it in order to craft an appropriate response for the reporter. The court wrote,

*Disbarment recognizes the seriousness of Cassilly's misconduct and serves the goal of protecting the public and ensuring the public's confidence in the legal profession by deterring other attorneys from engaging in similar misconduct.*

I tried to absorb one hundred and three pages of information. The court went even further than Judge Howe's opinion, finding a clear issue with Cassilly's refusal, as a duly elected officer of the court, to provide his testimony under oath. It was a scathing review by the court of appeals toward every one of the charges levied upon Cassilly. Their summation header was clear and direct,

*ATTORNEY DISCIPLINE - SANCTIONS - DISBARMENT* - Court of Appeals disbarred lawyer who, in his capacity as prosecutor, knowingly and intentionally failed to disclose for more than decade exculpatory evidence that came to light after defendant's conviction, discarded evidence, sought to have forensic evidence in case destroyed, knowingly made false statements of fact to court and defense counsel concerning content of evidence, and, during Bar Counsel's investigation, failed to comply with subpoena to provide statement under oath. Such conduct violated Maryland Attorneys' Rules of Professional Conduct 3.3(a)(1) (Candor Toward Tribunal), 3.4(a) (Fairness to Opposing Party and Counsel), 3.8(d) (Special Responsibilities of Prosecutor), 8.1(b)(Failing to Respond to Lawful Demand for Information), 8.4(c) (Dishonesty, Fraud, Deceit, or Misrepresentation), 8.4(d)(Conduct that is Prejudicial to Administration of Justice), and 8.4(a)(Violating Rules of Professional Conduct). (https://www.courts.state.md.us/data/opinions/coa/2021/31a20ag.pdf)

I juggled calls and texts while I absorbed the news. We went up against Goliath and succeeded beyond anyone's expectations. I wasn't prepared for this favorable outcome. It was never my experience for anyone to hear me or have the truth acknowledged. My legal and PR teams helped me come up with a short comment to share with the reporter. I joined the conference call where Chong, my lead attorney, and Tim Prudente awaited. Chong asked if I was sitting down., Prudente reached out to Cassilly for comment as well. Like me, Cassilly heard about the ruling from him and his response was, "Oh, whatever. I'm retired anyway. Do I care? I don't give a damn."

I was blown away. After a forty-year struggle that finally revealed the truth, this was to be the epitaph. No acceptance of wrongdoing, no acknowledgment or respect towards Maryland's highest court and their findings. No apology to me, the families of the victims, or to the citizens of Maryland who elected him to represent them for the past thirty-six years. It threw me off of my prepared statement. I responded, "He doesn't give a fuck. Doesn't care, never has. That's what we've been dealing with for forty years. He doesn't care what the judges say. He's got it in his head that he is the arresting officer, the prosecuting attorney, the judge, the jury, and, in my case, the executioner."

I went on to thank my attorneys, the Bar Counsel, and the courts, "This has been a forty-year journey. It started when I was 18, I'm 59 now. I've waited for the truth and for it to be told and heard. Today it was, and I'm very grateful."

I felt validated but emotionally I was spent. I was back out in the world for almost eight years at this point. While by most standards I'm considered successful, I've felt marginalized and not whole. My circle of friends and network of colleagues were supportive and non-judgmental. However, I still felt the need to explain myself, do more than average, and prove myself day after day. Every introduction included my background. I felt like I was an interesting dinner guest for an evening, but not normal enough for acceptance. Because of my criminal record, there were obstacles that prevented me from functioning in society the way everyone else did. I'm punished endlessly for a crime that I didn't commit.

While my life appears amazing on social media, it's truly the opposite. I struggle in my personal relationships, my financial well-being, navigating life, and finding my peace.

For a brief couple of days, I allowed this validation and the emotions of this victory to sweep me away. High fives and back-patting for lawyers and supporters who dedicated so much hard work and effort on my behalf. Also, a validation for my attorneys in their legal careers and for the profession as a whole. Cassilly's disbarment was only the fifth time in the United States that a prosecutor was disbarred for his conduct in a wrongful conviction case. Quite naturally, it exploded into national news.

It was easy to slide into the moment and get caught up in the excitement; to imagine that somehow everything would change. The reality is that the ruling didn't change my circumstances in the least. From the court's perspective, the disbarment of Cassilly punished the perpetrator. For me, it did nothing toward clearing my name or restoring lost decades. It didn't do anything to change my world.

A few weeks after the court's decision, my law firm and I held a national press conference to announce the filing of a petition for a pardon from Maryland's Governor, Larry Hogan. It came with the support and endorsement of several of the governor's cabinet members as well as many prominent business and community leaders. A petition for pardon is not necessarily the appropriate format. This is the final remedy. I'm no longer in the jurisdiction of the court system, where it should have been corrected in the first place. It seems unconscionable that after the court granted me the Writ of Actual Innocence the case was turned over to Cassilly. The very man and reason I was awarded the Writ in the first place was the person who decided what would happen next. After Cassilly's disbarment and the miscarriage of justice spotlighted, his successor could have fixed the situation by filing a Motion of Vacatur. He expressed to my attorneys that he disliked that particular law; therefore, he is content to wait and see if the Governor issues a pardon. The difference between the two is important. A Motion of Vacatur would clear this from my record once and for all, whereas the

Governor's pardon provides me with a piece of paper stating that I've received an innocent pardon.

That's where things stand. I still fight to clear my name and hope that day too, will come. Justice has a long way of working itself out and sometimes it takes eons. It took just short of forty years for this to happen for me. I saw this as validation for everything I've professed from day one. I am innocent of these charges. I was fortunate enough that I was able to outlive and outlast the situation.

I am grateful for the opportunities that allow me to share my story, which I try to do with a mission attached to it. Citizens need to be conscious of the criminal justice system because it does impact our daily lives whether we realize it or not. As a nation, we're building more prisons at taxpayers' expense. Doing so takes money away from both the community and education. The impact is exponential. It's incumbent upon us to understand our justice system and how it works, why it works, or why it doesn't work - and recognize when it's broken. And, trust me, with over 2.4 million people imprisoned in what we call mass incarceration, our system broke long ago.

That's an easy figure to talk about, 2.4 million. But what we don't talk about is the other 5 plus million who are on parole or probation out in our communities. This permeates pretty much every aspect of our society. I see it as a circle with three arcs.

The first arc represents the school-to-prison pipeline. It includes strategies to divert young people away from pathways that lead them to criminal behavior and thus, feed them into the criminal justice system.

The second arc of the circle represented the men and women in prison. At this time in America, 2.4 million individuals are incarcerated. What are we doing with them? Are we warehousing them? Are we providing them with substantive training, opportunity, or education? What about job training and job skills? These are crucial keys to ensuring that returning citizens find success upon release. It's critical that we don't make incarceration a waste of time. There is a punishment factor when incarceration removes convicts from their loved ones and everything that goes with it. It isn't necessary to go beyond that by adding on inhumane conditions, discouraging family or community relationships, limiting access to appropriate health care, abusing the use and implementation of solitary confinement, and abusing authority to physically beat up inmates. Warehousing and dehumanizing people will not produce productive citizens. Seventy-five percent of people in prison will get released. If we put our foot on their necks, then society pays for that in the end.

The third and final arc is what do we do when they come home? That is the lane where I have spent the majority of my professional career since coming home. Working with men and women to create successful re-entry and reintegration into society. The term returning citizen has come into popular use, referring to convicts who have returned to society as equal citizens. Most states now restore their voting rights and they pay taxes like any other citizen. Returnees should be contributing and supporting members of their communities. Yet there are still issues like hiring returning citizens and renting them an apartment. As easy as it sounds, a returning citizen can't simply fill out an application and live where they want. That scenario doesn't exist when a person has a record. There are background checks that preclude returning citizens from living in nice apartments. Then they become stuck in negative environments where the cycle of recidivism/incarceration continues. As a community, as a society, we need to figure out where returning citizens can fit in. Where can we contribute to affecting positive change? People can make a difference. The first step is being aware and educated. When people get upset about my story, I encourage them to find their voice and find where they can best have an impact.

I cannot quantify what impact my involvement in prison programming may have had on others. There were a lot of people who followed our path. Many of those young guys I spoke about are doing very well today. In fact, one ended up working for me as a case manager. He is another example of a prisoner who settled down, earned his college degree, and in the end, the governor commuted his life sentence. He was one of four lifers that the governor commuted. We never know when we throw a pebble what the ripple effects will be. For me, it felt like the right thing to do – to involve myself, to set an example, to help my community. I owed it to my parents, and I owed it to myself. I want to lead a fulfilled life for a lot of reasons. For myself and my parents first. Then I want to honor everyone who believed in me and fought for me. I carry a lot of weight on my shoulders to make sure that I not only do the right thing but that I'm successful at doing it. I live a very blessed life and feel like I get to do a lot of cool things. I have opportunities through my company's foundation, Kinetic Capital Community Foundation, to give back and have a positive impact on marginalized communities. I stand in the company of great friends and advocates like the legendary Jason Flom, Barry Scheck, and Laura Nirider. All of whom are bringing national attention to the issue of wrongful convictions. I am privileged to know Erica Suter, Marc Howard, and Marty Tankleff. Marty is an exoneree turned lawyer and law professor. There are several other attorneys and student volunteers who devoted countless hours of time and energy to fix those wrongs. I proudly wear my Death Row Exoneree ring created and crafted by Kirk Bloodsworth, the first person on death row in the United States, and my neighbor on the tier, exonerated by DNA. I am humbled to have these friendships and stand shoulder to shoulder with them in their efforts to correct obscene miscarriages of justice.

# About the Author

©Karen Elliot Greisdorf

John N. Huffington spent more than 32 years in the Maryland Prison System, 10 years of which were spent on Death Row.

Today, he is currently the Corporate Social Responsibility Director for Holdings Management Company. He serves as the Vice President & COO of the Kinetic Capital Community Foundation, a charitable organization headquartered in Maryland. Additionally, he supports and works in several charitable organizations throughout the state. In particular, John's work helps get food donations and school supplies.

Find John on social media via @HuffingtonJohn

CPSIA information can be obtained
at www.ICGtesting.com
Printed in the USA
LVHW011539241022
731425LV00009B/1112

9 798985 410822